Spreading the Word
Scottish Publishers and English Literature 1750–1900

Spreading the Word

Scottish Publishers and English Literature 1750–1900

Lionel Gossman

American Philosophical Society Press
Philadelphia

> Transactions of the
> American Philosophical Society
> Held at Philadelphia
> For Promoting Useful Knowledge
> Volume 109, Part 2

For some figures included in the text, higher-resolution images were unavailable.

Copyright © 2020 by the American Philosophical Society for its Transactions series.

All rights reserved.

ISBN: 978-1-60618-092-1
Ebook ISBN: 978-1-60618-097-6
US ISSN: 0065-9746

Library of Congress Cataloging-in Publication Data

Names: Gossman, Lionel, author.
Title: Spreading the word : Scottish publishers and English literature, 1750-1900 / Lionel Gossman.
Description: Philadelphia : American Philosophical Society Press, [2020] | Series: Transactions of the American Philosophical Society, 0065-9746; volume 109, part 2 | Includes bibliographical references and index. | Summary: "In view of the value placed in Scotland on education, reading, and self-improvement and the enterprise and inventiveness with which the inhabitants of the far poorer northern kingdom responded to the opportunities opened up to them by the Union with England, it is not surprising that Scotsmen were heavily represented in the printing and publishing trades. An altogether disproportionate number of the great publishing houses of the English-speaking world, whose names were to become household words - Blackie, Blackwood, Collins, Constable, Macmillan, Millar, Murray, Nelson, Smith and Elder, Strahan — were founded by men, often enough of quite humble origin, from "north of the border."—Provided by publisher.
Identifiers: LCCN 2019056887 (print) | LCCN 2019056888 (ebook) | ISBN 9781606180921 (paperback) | ISBN 9781606180976 (kindle edition)
Subjects: LCSH: Publishers and publishing—Scotland—History—18th century. | Publishers and publishing—Scotland—History—19th century. | English literature—Publishing—Scotland—History—18th century. | English literature—Publishing—Scotland—History—19th century.
Classification: LCC Z330.3.S36 G67 2020 (print) | LCC Z330.3.S36 (ebook) | DDC 070.509411/09033—dc23
LC record available at https://lccn.loc.gov/2019056887
LC ebook record available at https://lccn.loc.gov/2019056888

Also available as an ebook

Contents

Foreword   *vii*

Introduction: Scotland and the Modern World   *ix*

Scottish Publishers and English Letters   1

Index   *141*

Foreword

I planned and wrote part of this essay some time ago, in 2007 to be exact. I intended it to accompany an exhibition I had hoped to set up in Princeton University's Firestone Library in celebration of the 300th anniversary of the Union of the Scottish and English Parliaments. It turned out that the library's exhibition space was fully booked for the year, and so the plan fell through. At a time of growing uncertainty about the future of the Union, however, I believe the matter of the little essay remains of interest, even though the formal occasion for it has passed, and so I took it up again in December of 2017. The pages devoted to Scottish achievement in fields other than publishing reflect the original intention of the planned exhibition: namely, to draw viewers' attention to the benefits brought about by the integration of Scotland into the modern world, in large measure as a result of the Union and despite the relative unpopularity of the Union among ordinary Scots at the time. They also reflect, admittedly, my own patriotic feelings for the country in which I was born, raised, educated, and—during World War II—protected from harm.

Introduction: Scotland and the Modern World

With a population, in the mid-eighteenth century, of about a million and a quarter,[1] Scotland was a small and in many respects backward country on the outer rim of Europe, remote from the main centers of European power and influence, and endowed with few natural resources. Poor as it was, however, 17th- and 18th-century Scotland had one of the highest literacy rates in Europe.[2] The Reformation, which had been carried out in the spirit of Calvin and his Scottish disciple John Knox, encouraged all Christians to read Holy Scripture for themselves. Knox called for a national education system as early as 1560 and over the course of the seventeenth century (1616, 1633, and 1646) the Scottish Parliament passed various statutes purporting to institute one. As the measures mandated proved to be irregularly or inadequately executed, these earlier Acts were reinforced in 1696 by an "Act for Setting Schools," which required every parish in the country to supply a "commodious house for a school" and a salary for a schoolmaster or "dominie."[3] As a result, most Scottish children received at least a basic education, except in the sparsely populated, Gaelic-speaking Highlands—where the chief purpose of the various Acts was in fact to establish the use of "inglis" and stamp out Gaelic, viewed by the legislators as inseparably connected with the alleged barbarity and incivility of the speakers of that language. "In Scotland," according to Adam Smith, "the establishment of parish schools has taught almost the whole common people to read, and a very great proportion of them to write and account."[4] There is evidence of keen interest in books and reading. The records of Innerpeffray Library (founded in 1680 as a free lending library by David Drummond, 3rd Lord Madertie, near the small town of Crieff in Perthshire and still standing today) indicate that in the years between 1747 and 1800 its chief borrowers were the local baker, blacksmith, cooper, dyer, and dyer's apprentice, along with farmers, stonemasons, quarriers, tailors, and household servants, and that the books most heavily borrowed, besides collections of sermons and church histories, included the writings of Locke and Buffon, and—most popular of all—Robertson's *History of Charles V*.[5]

Libraries sprang up everywhere. It took many years before the Rev. James Kirkwood's *Overture for founding and maintaining of bibliothecks in every paroch throughout this Kingdom* of 1699 was fully realized,[6] but by the mid-18th century there were publicly accessible libraries of various kinds all over Scotland: privately owned libraries lending out books, subscribers' libraries founded and sustained by their members, a very early public library–the "Publick Liberarie" of Kirkwall in the remote Orkney Islands, to which a donor, one William Blake, bequeathed his personal library of over 150 books in 1683[7]—circulating libraries, the first of which in all Britain is traditionally held to have been established by the poet Allan Ramsay in Edinburgh in 1725, mechanics institutes' libraries, and even, by 1817, so-called "itinerating libraries," designed to meet the needs of the smallest villages by moving from one to another. In 1828 the "gratuitous librarians" of these traveling libraries included "a shoemaker, a draper, a labourer, a coalier, a baker, a tailor, a weaver, two saddlers, two smiths, three wrights and six teachers," according to the report of a Parliamentary Select Committee on public libraries in 1849.[8] Often, libraries were set up by the working people themselves. In 1749 the miners of Leadhills in Lanarkshire created the "large library of long standing" mentioned by Dorothy Wordsworth in her "Recollections" of a journey to Scotland with her brother William in 1803. The example of the Leadhill miners was followed seven years later by the miners in the neighboring village of Wanlockhead. Long before Andrew Carnegie began promoting and endowing libraries on a worldwide scale, other successful Scots were generous supporters of public libraries. The engineer Thomas Telford, for example, was "so much impressed with the advantages arising from libraries" that in 1834 he donated a substantial sum of money to those in the small Dumfriesshire town of Langholm and in the nearby village of Westerkirk, his birthplace, where a library had been instituted in 1792 by the miners at a local antimony mine. Telford stipulated that the interest on his two gifts was to be "annually laid out in the purchase of books." According to one rather romantic account from the middle of the 19th century, "readers of all ages and conditions—farmers, shepherds, ploughmen, labourers and their children—resort to [the Westerkirk library] from far and near, taking away with them as many volumes as they desire for the month's reading. Thus there is scarcely a cottage in the valley in which good books are not to be found under perusal; and we are told that it is a common thing for the Eskdale shepherd to take a book in his plaid to the hillside—a volume of Shakespeare, Prescott, or Macaulay—and read it there, under the blue sky, with his sheep and the green hills before him."[9] If some communities in Scotland were surprisingly slow to take advantage of an 1850 Act of Parliament (extended to Scotland in 1853) that allowed local authorities to levy a tax for the purpose of establishing and maintaining public libraries, this was probably due, as one historian has put it, "to the way Scotland is used to the private endowment of public foundations. The Scots are frugal and saving; but no people are more generous in works for the common weal. Hence it is not difficult to understand the reluctance of Glasgow to saddle itself with a library rate, when it already had its impressive Stirling's Library," founded by a local merchant in 1791, and its Baillie's Institution (1863) and Mitchell Library, founded in 1877 by Stephen Mitchell, a super-wealthy tobacco producer, and today "one of the largest public reference libraries in Europe,"[10] were both about to open. As will be seen in the descriptions of the individual publishing houses founded by Scots, the Scottish passion for diffusing knowledge and culture among the common people, along with a Presbyterian-based commitment to religion and morality (and a no less keen business sense), was a major inspiration of several of these houses—Constable, Murray, Macmillan, and most notable, Blackie, Collins, and Nelson.[11]

In addition to promoting literacy, it was one of the tenets of Calvinism that everyone should labor in the vineyard of the Lord—that is, do everything possible to maintain and embellish the world that the Lord had created. For Calvinists, one might say, work was a form of worship. With the Act of Union, which united the parliaments of Scotland and England in 1707 (until then the two countries had been not only independent, albeit sharing a single monarch since 1603, but frequently at war with one another) a vast field of new opportunities was opened up to the ambitious "lad o'pairts," the talented youngster nurtured by the relatively democratic Scottish education system. Of these the inhabitants of what was now often referred to as "North Britain" took full advantage. That is the reality behind Dr. Johnson's celebrated and meanly intended quip (in July, 1763) that "the noblest prospect which a Scotchman ever sees, is the high road that leads him to England."

In nearly every field of human endeavor, Scots began to spread their wings. In philosophy, Hutcheson, Hume, and the later "Scottish Common Sense School" (Reid, Beattie, Dugald Stewart) exercised enormous influence on philosophers and educators throughout Europe and North America. In literature, Boswell created one of the greatest biographies of all time and Burns a modern poetry in the vernacular that won devotees all over the world. Scott invented and launched the vogue of the historical novel, achieving unprecedented international popularity. In economics, it is unnecessary to emphasize the founding contribution of Adam Smith, a graduate of Glasgow University and subsequently Professor of Moral Philosophy there. In the social sciences, David Hume and William Robertson, the Principal of Edinburgh University, were regarded by contemporaries as the leading British historians, on a par with Gibbon, while Edinburgh University's Adam Ferguson (*The History of Civil Society*, 1768) and Glasgow University's John Millar (*Origin of the Distinction of Ranks*, 1779; *A Historical View of the English Government*, 1787)—all three books quickly translated into French and German—are generally viewed as having laid the foundations of modern historical sociology. Karl Marx, among others, was an admirer and assiduous reader of both Ferguson and Millar.

In chemistry, the experiments of Joseph Black at Glasgow in 1755 led to the concept of latent heat, helped to undermine the then prevalent "phlogiston" theory, and directed other British scientists toward the chemical nature of gases. Unlike his English contemporaries Priestley and Cavendish, Black immediately accepted the work of Lavoisier and incorporated it into his teaching. In the following century Clerk Maxwell (1831–79) made contributions to theoretical physics that Einstein was to describe as "the most profound and the most fruitful that physics has experienced since the time of Newton." The Scots–Irish William Thomson (1824–1907), later Lord Kelvin, appointed Professor of Natural Philosophy at the University of Glasgow at the age of 22, laid the foundations of modern thermodynamics, besides being a significant inventor on the side. (He helped to design the first transatlantic submarine cable). In 1795 James Hutton's *Theory of the Earth* gave a new impetus to geology by initiating systematic empirical study of the history of the planet.

Among the many celebrated Scottish physicians in the eighteenth century the two Hunter brothers from Glasgow were among the most influential in the development of medical practice. Along with another Scot, William Smellie, William Hunter helped to turn obstetrics into a scientifically precise discipline; his brother John did the same for dentistry and surgery. By the mid-18th century medical education at Edinburgh, thoroughly grounded in empirical study and hands-on practice, was considered superior to anything available in England, and it was to Edinburgh that, on Benjamin Franklin's advice, Benjamin Rush, a graduate of the College of New Jersey, traveled to study for his M.D. On his return to Philadelphia, as is well known, Rush laid the foundations of medical education in the thirteen colonies. The first black American to earn a medical degree anywhere in the world, James McCune Smith, obtained it at Glasgow in 1837.[12] In the 19th and 20th centuries Scottish physicians continued to make significant contributions to medicine. In 1847 James Young Simpson, professor of midwifery at Edinburgh, published his groundbreaking account of the use of chloroform in surgical anesthesia; in the early 1860s surgeons from all over the world came to Joseph Lister's ward at the Royal Infirmary in Glasgow, where the English-born Lister had been appointed Professor of Surgery, to observe his pioneering, life-saving use of antiseptic in surgical operations; in 1923 John Richard Macleod, a graduate of Aberdeen, received the Nobel prize in medicine for his contribution to the discovery of insulin; in 1928 Alexander Fleming, based in London but born and educated in Ayrshire, first observed the effects of penicillin; in the 1950s Ian Donald, Regius Professor of Midwifery at Glasgow, pioneered the use of diagnostic ultrasound; in 1988 James W. Black was awarded a Nobel prize for his discovery of beta-blockers. All in all, Scots have won up to 10% of Nobel prizes in the sciences—no mean achievement for a nation with a population of only a million and a half in 1801 and five million in 2001.

Scottish engineers and inventors did not lag behind their academic or medical fellow-countrymen. With help and encouragement from Joseph Black and using space provided by Glasgow University, James Watt vastly improved on early versions of the steam engine and founded a company to build and market his machines. John Loudon Macadam revolutionized roadbuilding. Thomas Telford also made major improvements to roadbuilding techniques and designed the first modern suspension bridge, the beautiful Menai bridge (1819–26), linking Wales and the island of Anglesey. John Broadwood, a cabinetmaker from the Lothians, transformed an eighteenth-century London harpsichord workshop into the great piano making company that still exists today, patented several improvements to the piano's design, and won the favor of Haydn and Beethoven. In the early nineteenth century Charles Macintosh invented waterproof fabric, making life easier for millions—not least in his native country, where rainwater is the one plentiful natural resource. Around 1834 James Chalmers devised the adhesive postage stamp and proposed a uniform, nationwide postal rate. Twelve years later, Robert Thomson, from Stonehaven in the Northeast of Scotland, patented a pneumatic tire and, three years after that, a fountain pen. In 1875 Scots-born and Edinburgh-educated Alexander Graham Bell invented and patented the telephone. A decade later, John Boyd Dunlop devised the first practical pneumatic tire (further improved the following year by the American-born director of the North British Rubber Company of Edinburgh, William Erskine Bartlett) and began commercial production in 1890. Also in the 1890s James Dewar invented the thermos flask. In 1926 John Logie Baird of Helensburgh, a commuter town on the Firth of Clyde down river from Glasgow, gave the first public demonstration of television in the world, with transmission of color images and transatlantic transmission coming just two years later. In 1935 Robert Watson-Watt invented the first workable radar system.

Very early in the nineteenth century, Henry Bell, developing earlier designs by fellow-Scot William Symington, built the first commercially viable steamboat in Europe and by 1812 had it running regular passenger service between Glasgow and Greenock. Not long afterward William Fairbairn pioneered the construction of iron-hulled ships. By the end of the century Glasgow and Clydeside had become the greatest centers of shipbuilding and naval engineering in the world. Meanwhile, Scottish entrepreneurs were active everywhere from North America, where Andrew Carnegie dominated the steel industry, to East Asia, where William Jardine and James Matheson had the more dubious distinction of cornering the immensely profitable opium trade. Scots were also leading explorers (James Bruce, David Livingstone, Mungo Park, Alexander Mackenzie, and John Rae, discoverer of the North Magnetic Pole), as well as administrators and governors-general of the territories of the expanding British Empire (Thomas Brisbane, Ronald Ferguson, John Hope, and Lachlan Macquarie in Australia; David Boyle and James Ferguson in New Zealand; James Bruce, Gilbert Elliott, John Macpherson, James Ramsay, and Victor Hope in India; most recently John Buchan, the novelist, and before him James Bruce, John Campbell, James Henry Craig, Gordon Drummond, Gilbert Elliott, John Hamilton-Gordon in Canada).[13]

NOTES

1. According to the 1755 census of the Rev. Alexander Webster, usually considered fairly reliable (https://www.nrscotland.gov.uk/research/guides/census-records/webster%E2%80%99s-census-of-1755).
2. Harvey J. Graff, *The Legacies of Literacy: Continuities and Contradictions in Western European Culture and Society* (Bloomington: Indiana University Press, 1987), 169, fig. 5.6; 375, fig. E.1. This generally held view has lately been subjected to close scrutiny. In *Scottish Literacy and the Scottish Identity: Illiteracy and Society in Scotland and Northern England 1600–1800* (Cambridge: Cambridge University Press, 1985), R. A. Houston, a professor at St. Andrews University, observes that there is in fact not much hard evidence for the traditional and often repeated claim about high Scottish literacy. He implies that the claim has much to do with Scottish self-perception and sense of national identity. His view is contested by T. C. Smout, also of St. Andrews, who distinguishes reading and writing ability and argues from a persuasive sample that reading ability was effectively at 100% among the common people ("Born Again at Cambuslang: New Evidence on Popular Religion and Literacy in Eighteenth-Century Scotland," *Past and Present, 97* [1982]: 114–27, here 121–27). For a still more recent reading of the literacy claim, see the editors' Introduction in Stephen W. Brown and Warren McDougall, eds., *The Edinburgh History of the Book in Scotland*, vol. 2, "Enlightenment and Expansion 1707–1800" (Edinburgh: Edinburgh University Press, 2012), 18–19; and Mark R. M. Towsey, *Reading the Scottish Enlightenment* (Leiden: Brill, 2010), 16n56.
3. See: https://en.wikipedia.org/wiki/School_Establishment_Act_1616 https://en.wikipedia.org/wiki/Education_Act_1633 https://en.wikipedia.org/wiki/Education_Act_1646 https://en.wikipedia.org/wiki/Education_Act_1696
4. Adam Smith, *An Inquiry into the Nature and Causes of the Wealth of Nations*, Book V, ch. 1, part III, article 2 (New York: The Modern Library, 1937), 737. See, however, T. C. Smout

(see note 2), who found writing ability notably less widespread than reading ability among the common people.

5. Paul Kaufman, "Innerpeffray: Reading for all the People," in his *Libraries and their Users. Collected Papers in Library History* (London: The Library Association, 1969), 154–55.

6. On Kirkwood's proposal, which was intended for the General Assembly of the Church of Scotland, see Kaufman, "Scotland as the Home of Community Libraries," *Libraries and their Users* (as in note 5), 140–41. Also W. R. Aitken, *A History of the Public Library Movement in Scotland* (Glasgow: The Scottish Library Association, 1971), 6–10.

7. On the Kirkwall Bibliotheck, see http://orkneyarchive.blogspot.com/p/history.html See also Aitken (as in note 6), 2–5. Aitken recalls, however (1–2), that a century earlier, in 1580, an advocate in Edinburgh, one Clement Little, left "ane sufficient nummer of guid and godlie buikis to the ministrie of this burgh" in the hope that it would inspire similar bequests, "quhairby it may follow that ane commoun Librarie sall be erectit within this burgh." Access, however, was to be free to persons willing to "trauell and be excercised in the estait and vocation of ministerie."

8. Cited in Aitken (as in note 6), 31n107.

9. Samuel Smiles, *Lives of the Engineers*, vol. 2, cited in Thomas Kelly, *Public Libraries in Great Britain before 1850* (London: The Library Association, 1966), 210.

10. Ernest A. Baker, *The Public Library* (London: Grafton, 1924), 23. For a richly documented and comprehensive overview of libraries in Scotland in the eighteenth and early nineteenth centuries, see especially Towsey, *Reading the Scottish Enlightenment* (as in note 2), 23–159; and Aitken, *A History of the Public Library Movement in Scotland* (as in note 6).

11. An additional, suggestive consideration has been put forward by Stephen W. Brown and Warren McDougall in the Introduction to their edited volume 2 of *The Edinburgh History of the Book in Scotland* (as in note 2): Scotland "was a literate nation in ways that went far beyond any measurable achievement of its educational system. Literacy provided Scotland with economic opportunities of a sophisticated kind in which the

English language itself became a product. What Scotland mostly read in the eighteenth century was not printed in the language of daily life. Scots was spoken, English read, and something of what it meant to be British in Scotland was expressed by that duality. Thus, although Scotland's courts were unlike England's in their requirement that pleas, charges, defenses, and decisions be not only written down, but printed and published, those texts were in English, not the Scots of actual courtroom discourse. A respect for the bureaucratic importance of literacy among Scotland's legal community consequently became the bedrock of Edinburgh's printers. [. . .] Scottish literacy after 1707 increasingly meant being at ease with spoken and written English. To this end *belles-lettres* became something of an industry and the reprinters gave their countrymen cheaper editions of Milton, Addison, Swift, Pope, Johnson and, of course, Shakespeare." Plays, in particular, being both shorter and cheaper to print than novels, and directly contributing to language fluency were "the single greatest source of material for Scottish literary reprints throughout the period" (20–21).

12. See *Avenue* (the magazine of the Glasgow University Alumni Association), June 2002 and May 2017. A major new building at Glasgow University, named in his honor the "James McCune Smith Learning Hub," is due to open 2019–20.

13. It is only right to acknowledge that the record of Scottish achievement, viewed from our contemporary perspective, is by no means unblemished. The role of the slave trade in the enrichment of the merchants of Glasgow and of the University of Glasgow itself through the so-called "triangular trade" in people, sugar, tobacco, and later cotton—long suppressed in Scotland's image of itself as a deeply democratic culture—has lately entered Scottish self-awareness (https://www.nts.org.uk/learn/downloads/Scotland%20and%20the%20SlaveTrade.pdf), become a significant topic of research among historians, including Scottish historians (e.g., Stephen Mullen, *It Wisnae Us: The Truth about Glasgow Slavery* [Edinburgh: The Royal Incorporation of Architects in Scotland, 2009]; Carla Sassi and Theo van Hejns-

bergen, eds., *Within and Without Empire: Scotland across the (Post)colonial Borderline* [Newcastle-on-Tyne: Cambridge Scholars, 2013]; Michael Morris, *Scotland and the Caribbean c. 1740–1830* [New York: Routledge, 2015]), and inspired the University of Glasgow to make partial atonement for its historical links to the transatlantic slave trade by donating £20 million for the establishment, in co-operation with the University of the West Indies, of an institute for the study of slavery. Among the governors-general of India, James Bruce, Eighth Earl of Elgin (1862–63) ordered the destruction of the Summer Palace in Peking, an act of extraordinary vandalism that the military situation in no way required; James Ramsay, 1st Marquis of Dalhousie (1848–1856), the so-called "maker of modern India" through the introduction of railways, a uniform postal service, and the education of broader sections of the population, including women, is often held responsible for the authoritarianism and oppressive measures against native Indian rulers that incited the Indian Uprising of 1857; Victor Hope (1936–43) has been held accountable for the Bengal famine of 1943.

Scottish Publishers and English Letters

> If asked, why Printers and Booksellers in particular?—I answer, they are a valuable class of the community—the friendly assistants, if not the patrons of literature.
>
> —John Nichols (writer and printer, 1745–1826, cited on title page of C. H. Timperley, *A Dictionary of Printers and Printing* (London: H. Johnson, 1839)[1]

In view of the value placed in Scotland on education, reading, and self-improvement and the enterprise and inventiveness with which the inhabitants of the far poorer northern kingdom responded to the opportunities opened up to them by the union with England, it is not surprising that Scotsmen were heavily represented in the printing and publishing trades. An altogether disproportionate number of the great publishing houses of the English-speaking world, whose names were to become household words—Blackie, Blackwood, Collins, Constable, Macmillan, Millar, Murray, Nelson, Smith and Elder, Strahan—were founded by men, often enough of quite humble origin, from "north of the border."[2] The *Encyclopaedia Britannica* (1768–71) was the brainchild of two Edinburgh men: Colin Macfarquhar, a printer, and Andrew Bell, an engraver. Characteristically, the 28-year old printer's apprentice they entrusted with putting together and editing the first edition, William Smellie (1740–95), was a largely self-educated polymath, who at the age of 19 had prepared an edition of Terence that won a prize for his employer from the Edinburgh

Philosophical Society. (The same Smellie went on to be a respected naturalist and antiquary and co-founder of both the Royal Society of Edinburgh and the Society of Antiquaries of Scotland.)

Though many, but by no means all, the Scottish publishers began by publishing official and legal documents and religious works, they soon extended their activities to belles-lettres, including cheap editions of the ancient classics and of major modern writers, as well as to history, writings on science, medicine, philosophy, politics, and economics; accounts of travel and exploration; practical manuals of everything from engineering to gardening; and popular encyclopedias and other reference works, such as the still ongoing Grove's *Dictionary of Music* (first put out by Macmillan in four volumes between 1877 and 1889) and specialized journals such as *Nature* (also put out by Macmillan and ongoing since 1869). In the 18th and early 19th centuries, when the roles of printer, publisher, and bookseller were still fluid and overlapping, some went into publishing from the printing trade, others from bookselling. In most cases, printers also continued their printing business. Probably it was a more reliable source of steady income than publishing or owning shares in a publishing venture. Some, such as Millar, Murray, Strahan and, at a slightly later date, Smith and Elder or Macmillan, set up business in the South right away; others started out in Scotland but opened branch offices in London in order to reach a wider market, and then finally moved their main offices south; others still, like Blackie, Collins, Constable, and Nelson, managed to combine a worldwide reach with faithfulness to their Scottish origin. Writing in 1819, the heyday of publishing in Edinburgh, Walter Scott's son-in-law John Gibson Lockhart, a prolific writer himself, could claim—not, to be sure, without some exaggeration—that

> instead of Scotch authors sending their works to be published by London booksellers, there is nothing more common nowadays than to hear of English authors sending down their books to Edinburgh to be published in a city than which Memphis or Palmyra could scarcely have seemed a more absurd place of publication to any English author thirty years ago. One that has not examined into the matter would scarcely be able to believe how large a proportion of the classical works of English literature, published in our age, have made their first appearance on the counters of the Edinburgh booksellers. But [...] we all know that at this moment an Edinburgh title-page is better than any London one—and carries a greater authority along with it.[3]

Modern British copyright law was largely developed as a result of the activities of Scottish publishers (and the lawyers who defended them). Traditionally, publishers—who, as noted, were still also printers and booksellers—bought and sold shares in the works not only of contemporary writers but of classic writers like Shakespeare or Bacon, their investment being protected by a Licensing of the Press Act of 1662 that defined the property so acquired as being held, like landed property, in perpetuity and that was enforced by the publishers themselves, banded together as the officially recognized and empowered Stationers' Company, a central aim of which was to obstruct the sale of "pirated" editions. Copyright in perpetuity was not, however, recognized in Scottish law and, especially after the Union in 1707, which opened a wide market to the Scots, printers and booksellers north of the border turned out more and more editions of works that their London counterparts considered "pirated" and, as they were sold at lower prices, a serious danger to their own financial stability. Following Parliament's refusal in 1694 to renew the 1662 Act, the so-called Statute of Anne of 1710 provided publishers with protection of the literary property or shares they had acquired for a stipulated number of years. Copyright in perpetuity was thus no longer protected by positive law. Scottish booksellers and publishers disagreed with their English counterparts, however, about conditions after protection had lapsed, the former maintaining that the texts were thereafter in the public domain throughout the kingdom, the latter that although the penalties for infringement of copyright were no longer fixed but subject to review, copyright itself, holding the property of a literary work, like a landed property, in perpetuity, was still protected according to English common law, even if it was no longer protected by positive law.[4]

A series of lawsuits ensued in the 1760s and 1770s involving London booksellers and printer-publishers—not least among them a prominent Scot, Andrew Millar, together with his English apprentice, then partner and, finally, successor as head of the firm, Thomas Cadell—and, principally, Alexander Donaldson, one of the most successful of many Edinburgh booksellers and publishers of cheap, allegedly "pirated" editions of classic and popular works, which he sold not only in Scotland but in the North of England and in London itself at steeply discounted prices.[5] (His brother John had a bookstore in London and in the early 1770s he himself succeeded in opening a store of his own in St. Paul's Churchyard.) The London booksellers won in the English courts. But in 1773, at the Court of Session in Edinburgh (the Scottish High Court), where—with help from none other than James Boswell—Donaldson defended himself in a suit brought against him by the London bookseller and publisher John Hinton, the judgment of the court was in favor of Donaldson.[6] More significant, Donaldson again carried the day in 1774 in the House of Lords, to which two bills of complaint brought against him and his brother in 1771 by the London publishers John Rivington and Thomas Becket (a sometime apprentice of Andrew Millar) for printing and selling copies of two novels by Fielding had made their way from the Court of Chancery. The issue was essentially one of free trade versus protectionism and state control. William Strahan, a native of Edinburgh, who, like Millar, had moved south and set up business in London, deplored the success of "your little dirty pitiful Pyrates," as he put it in a letter to William Creech, a printer-publisher in Edinburgh.[7] (On Strahan, see pp. 10–12.) Unrestrained competition, Strahan maintained, would result in the ruin of publishing altogether: "I am only concerned for the trade in general, which must soon be destroyed," he wrote to Creech, "if every body is permitted to print every Thing. And if the Cause of Literary Property is decided against Perpetual Property or if the decision is long deferred, [...] I think the sooner you look out for another Occupation, the better. It will become quickly the most pitiful, beggarly, precarious, unprofitable, and disreputable Trade in Britain."[8] Perhaps it is not surprising that directly contrary views were expressed by the Scottish printer and publisher Robert Foulis, the official Printer of the College of Glasgow (where Adam Smith was Professor of Moral Philosophy) and a highly regarded printer-publisher of both ancient and modern works of literature in his own right. (On the Foulis Press, see pp. 12–15.) "Take away competition between buyers, and goods become cheap. Take away competition among sellers, and goods become dear," he wrote in a *Memorial of the Printers and Booksellers of Glasgow, Most Humbly Addressed to the Honourable House of Commons* in 1774. Foulis's argument, as summarized in a recent scholarly publication, is worth repeating here:

> As long as monopolies held sway consumers were unable to reap the benefits of "free competition," that is, "a contention for cheapness, for correctness, for elegance, for legibility." If, on the other hand, books were "more universally" printed, they would be more universally purchased and read. The taste for books in Scotland had spread on account of its reprint trade, and from Dublin itself [a center of unrestricted publishing—L. G.], Foulis wagered, London booksellers gained as much as they lost by the Irish reprint trade, because "wherever printing takes place, it diffuses the taste for books wider." A market that attracted more book buyers would generate more customers able to afford prestigious London editions. Thus, to re-instate the monopoly would perversely depress "honest industry among the whole body of London booksellers themselves," not to mention "its restraint on the industry of every printer and bookseller" outside of London. In sum, Foulis derided the idea that reprinting elsewhere in Britain in "any way ostensibly hurts the London trade." The principal injury to their economic interests was self-inflicted; they "diminish[ed] their own trade by endeavouring to bind the hands of their brethren all over the kingdom, who, if free and independent, would be able to trade with them more extensively, and on more equitable terms. [...]
>
> Aside from economic benefits, Foulis predicted a boon for scholarship as well. Come the day "when great authors can be printed with classical freedom," he hoped that competition would ensue not just among publishers to produce the cheapest or most legible books, but also among editors "to explain obscure passages

by their comments, correct mistakes by their notes, and supply defects by their additions taken from later discoveries." [...]

If Thomson [James Thomson— L. G.] and Chaucer were (as Foulis desired) more universally printed, they could be (as Thomas Warton wanted) more universally read. Classical freedom, could it be realized, would boost supply and demand alike.[9]

The outcome of the seemingly endless disputes and court cases involving publishers in Scotland and publishers in London (including those Scots active in the British capital) was not only a complete overhaul of traditional copyright law and its remaking into something closer to what still exists today, but a vast expansion of the book trade and of the reading public and—since old books were no longer protected by copyright and money could be made (or lost) chiefly through publication or shares in the publication of new books—the gradual separation of book printing, publishing, and selling into distinct commercial enterprises, even if some publishers, such as Collins and Nelson, still retained important printing facilities that they used to turn out inexpensive, mass-produced copies of established modern classics.[10] In addition, the new circumstances facilitated the rise, in Scotland, of important and productive publishing houses that, for a time, transformed the Scottish capital especially into a significant rival of London, where many of these houses established branch offices before spreading out to the British colonies (India, Australia, New Zealand, South Africa) and to the United States. Thomas Nelson of Edinburgh was the first British publisher to open a New York office, at 42 Bleeker Street, in 1854.

None of the great firms founded by Scots in the eighteenth and nineteenth centuries was able to resist the mergers and takeovers of the late twentieth century. A number of interesting and imaginative publishing houses have opened in Scotland recently, but they are small and are not remotely comparable in influence with the great houses set up in the eighteenth and nineteenth centuries. The following brief notes on the Scottish publishers are intended to bring into focus and draw attention to a remarkable achievement that has so far been recognized only in a few specialist studies of the book trade and that may well have been due in considerable measure to the particular combination of religion (in its Calvinist and Presbyterian form), enlightenment, and entrepreneurial spirit characteristic of eighteenth- and nineteenth- century Scotland and to the opportunities presented by the union with England.

MAJOR SCOTTISH PUBLISHING HOUSES

As noted briefly in the preceding text, publishing was for many years not independent of other aspects of book production and trade, but was largely in the hands of printers and booksellers. Several of these often acted as partners in the launching of a new book or bought and sold shares in an existing publication. Thus John Murray, William Strahan, and Thomas Cadell, who succeeded Andrew Millar on his death in 1768, frequently worked together. Edinburgh publisher Archibald Constable and short-lived London publisher Hurst, Robinson, or Edinburgh publisher William Blackwood and London publisher Thomas Cadell were frequently listed together on the title page of novels as the publishers for whom the book had been printed, the order of the listing no doubt indicating the primary and secondary partner.[11] Some Edinburgh-based publishers acted as agents for London-based publishers, and vice versa. The Murrays and the Constables, for instance, entertained close personal and business relationships for a time and John Murray II served for some years as Archibald Constable's London agent for the influential *Edinburgh Review*, which Constable launched in 1802. This did not prevent Murray from launching, seven years later—with the help of Constable's sometime author Walter Scott—the London-based, Tory-inclined *Quarterly Review*, which was specifically designed to compete with Constable's Whig-leaning journal. There was cooperation as well as competition among the publishers and it is widely recognized that the rival journals founded by Constable and Murray contributed to the creation of a new style of literary criticism in the United Kingdom.

The notes on some of the chief Scottish publishing houses that follow have been laid out in roughly chronological order. Major works in a wide range of fields, such as James Frazer's *Golden Bough* (Macmillan, 1890), emerged from the businesses founded by the Scots. Nevertheless, although I fully recognize that, before the Romantics, the category of belles-lettres included historical, political, philosophical, and even scientific writings, the focus in the following pages, in accordance with the title of the essay and with our current idea of literature, is chiefly, though by no means exclusively, on the role of the Scottish publishing houses in promoting and popularizing works that have become part of the literary canon.

*** **** ***

Andrew Millar (London) 1728

Born in 1705, the third of fourteen children of a Presbyterian minister in Port Glasgow, Andrew Millar was apprenticed at the age of fifteen to Edinburgh bookseller James McEuen; two years later he was employed at McEuen's branch in the Strand, in London; and in 1728 he was able to take the London shop over himself. From 1741 on, he was also the London agent for the Foulis Press (q.v.) of Glasgow. As a publisher, Millar acquired shares in classic texts by Milton and Francis Bacon, as well as in the Rev. Thomas Birch's expanded translation of Pierre Bayle's famous *Dictionary* (1734–41). He was the publisher of the first complete edition of James Thomson's celebrated four-part poem *The Seasons* (1730), as well as of works by many other Scots, among them the three volumes of *Essays and Treatises* (1753) and the *History of England* (1761) by his friend David Hume, the historian William Robertson's *History of Scotland* (1759), and the novelist Tobias Smollett's many novels. He was also the publisher of Smollett's translations of Le Sage's *Gil Blas* and Cervantes's *Don Quixote*, of Fielding's novels (*Tom Jones* [1741], *Joseph Andrews* [1751], *Amelia* [1752], and *Jonathan Wild* [1754]), and of the *Works* of Fielding in four volumes (1762); and he was a member of the syndicate of booksellers who financed Samuel Johnson's *Dictionary* in 1755. "I respect Millar," Dr. Johnson said of him in 1755, "he has raised the price of literature." (Millar paid Thomson £105 for *The Seasons*, Fielding £700 for *Tom Jones* and £1000 for *Amelia*.)

Scot though he was, Millar had set up his business in London and it was he who led the Stationers' war against allegedly "pirated" Scottish reprints with a series of lawsuits in the Scottish Court of Session, notably *Millar v. Kincaid* in 1743, on behalf of sixteen London bookseller-publishers against twenty Edinburgh-based and four Glasgow-based booksellers. When the Scottish Court ruled in this case that the Londoners' claimed copyright could not be protected, Millar appealed the decision to the House of Lords, where the Scottish Court's decision was upheld.[12] Millar did win an important victory in *Millar v. Taylor* (Court of King's Bench 1766–69), in which it was again argued on behalf of the plaintiff that authors and publishers are entitled to a perpetual common law copyright. But that posthumous decision (Millar died in London on June 8, 1768) was soon overturned in the landmark 1774 case of *Donaldson v. Beckett* (see p. 4).[13]

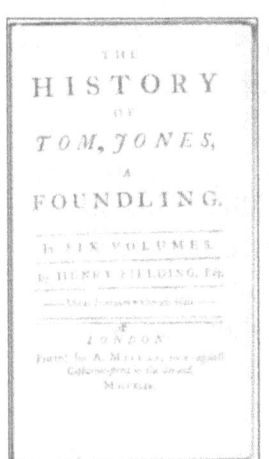

After Millar's death, the business was run by his former apprentice and subsequent partner, Thomas Cadell. In collaboration with William Strahan (q.v.), another Scot and sometime fellow-apprentice at Millar's, Cadell published Gibbon's *Decline and Fall of the Roman Empire* (1776–88), Johnson's *A Journey to the Western Islands of Scotland* (1775), Adam Smith's *The Wealth of Nations* (1776), as well as the poetry of Robert Burns (1787; the first edition having been put out by John Wilson of Kilmarnock in 1786 and then by William Creech of Edinburgh in 1787). Cadell was one of a group of booksellers who convinced Samuel Johnson to write his *Lives of the Most Eminent English Poets* (1779–81). Cadell also brought out many novels, including works by Tobias Smollett and the women writers Fanny Burney, Charlotte Smith, and—in translation—Mme de Graffigny and Mme de Genlis.

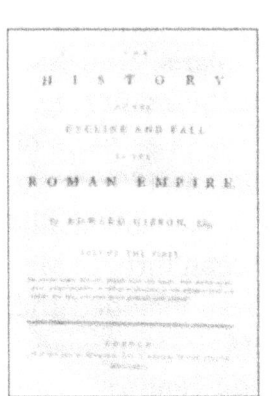

William Strahan (London) 1738

William Strachan, born in Edinburgh in April 1715 and educated at Edinburgh High School, served an apprenticeship as a journeyman printer in the Scottish capital before taking "the high road to England," where he was employed as a compositor for a London printer from May 1736 until February 1738. By November of that year, dropping the "c" from his name to make it appear less Scottish, Strahan was in the printing business himself, with one press. In that first year he got work from eight clients, including printer, publisher, and fellow-Scot Andrew Millar, his former employer [q.v.], who became Strahan's best customer, increasing his orders steadily every year until his death in 1768.

Thus, after Millar became Fielding's publisher, around 1742, Strahan began printing his works and by 1779 had printed almost 63,000 copies. He also printed over 20,000 copies of Thomson's hugely successful *Seasons* for Millar and almost as many of Hume's *Essays* and his popular *History of England*. By 1754 Strahan had nine presses going and was responsible for printing Johnson's *Dictionary* for Millar. He likewise became the chief printer for Thomas Becket, a former apprentice of Millar's, who had opened a publishing firm of his own. James Macpherson's *Fingal* (1763), Sterne's *Sermons of Mr. Yorick* (1760), as well as parts of *Tristram Shandy* (1760–67) and *A Sentimental Journey* (1768) were among the books printed by Strahan for Becket. Strahan finally entered publishing himself by buying up more than forty of Millar's titles after the latter's death in 1768. These included the works of John Locke and Adam Smith's *Theory of Moral Sentiments* (1759). He also collaborated in many publishing ventures with Millar's successor, Thomas Cadell, who became, in addition, the most important client of Strahan's printing business. In 1771 Strahan took a share with the author in an Edinburgh publication of Macpherson's *Fingal* and with Cadell in Henry Mackenzie's popular novel *The Man of Feeling*, which went through eight editions by 1781 and sold many thousands of copies. The year 1775 saw the publication of Johnson's *A Journey to the Western Islands of Scotland* and 1776 that of Adam Smith's *The Wealth of Nations*, both once again in collaboration with Millar's successor

Cadell, as well as of the first volume of Gibbon's *Decline and Fall of the Roman Empire* (which had been turned down by other publishers and for which Strahan doubled the fee Cadell had offered the author).

Strahan was a personal friend of many of the writers he published: Hume (who made him his literary executor in a codicil to his will in April 1776), Smith, Johnson, Gibbon, and Mackenzie. One of his visitors from Scotland—one Dr. Thomas Somerville, a minister in Jedburgh and subsequently the author of a *History of Great Britain during the Reign of Queen Anne* (1798)—describes going to dinner at Strahan's in 1769 and finding gathered there David Hume, the eminent Scottish physician John Pringle (soon to be appointed physician to George III), Benjamin Franklin, and Johnson's friend Mrs. (Hester) Thrale. The relationship with Franklin was especially close. It was on Strahan's recommendation that in 1743 Franklin brought Strahan's young friend and former fellow-apprentice in Edinburgh, David (Davie) Hall, yet another Scot, to Philadelphia to serve as his assistant in his printing shop. Hall soon became a partner, taking over the day-to-day running of the shop early in 1748, and taking it over completely in 1766 when the partnership with Franklin was dissolved.[14] Though severely tested at the time of the American War of Independence—Strahan, who had strong political interests and had won (or purchased) a seat in Parliament in 1774, understood the grievances of the American colonists, but strongly opposed their armed revolt and supported the British government's attempts to put it down—the friendship of the two men survived and was renewed after the end of the war.

Strahan's portrait was painted by Reynolds—an indication of the eminent place the printer-publisher occupied in the culture of his time. It was first exhibited in 1783, shortly before Strahan died, and is now part of the collection of the National Portrait Gallery in London.

On Strahan's death in 1785, the business was carried on by the youngest of his three sons, and on the death in 1831 of Andrew Strahan, who had no children of his own, by Andrew's nephew by marriage, Andrew Spottiswoode, the scion of an old Scottish family. The firm then tended, however, to concentrate on printing—government reports, scientific, political, and economic writings, and, on commission from the publishers, some literary works (by Robert Browning, Robert Louis Stevenson, and Fenimore Cooper, among others).

Robert and Andrew Foulis, The Foulis Press (Glasgow) 1741

Born in Glasgow in 1707, the son of a barber and maltman, and apprenticed in his turn to a barber, Robert Foulis practiced the trade as a master barber until 1738. He managed, however, to attend classes at Glasgow University (then generally known as "the College") and, as of 1730, enrolled in courses taught by the professor of moral philosophy, Francis Hutcheson, one of the founding fathers, along with Hume, Smith, and Ferguson, of the Scottish Enlightenment. He also took classes in Latin and Greek literature. Hutcheson thought well enough of his student to appoint him a tutor in his classes, and it may well have been Hutcheson who encouraged him to become a printer and bookseller and thus spread the "zeal for classical learning," shared by teacher and student, among the wider population. Robert Foulis's younger brother Andrew had a more formal education. He studied Humanity (still today the Scottish universities' term for "Latin") at the university, and later taught Greek, Latin, and French in Glasgow. He even applied—unsuccessfully—for the chair in Greek at the university.[15]

In 1738 while on a trip to France, the brothers purchased a number of books, exported them to Britain, and successfully sold them in London and Glasgow. Three years later Robert opened a bookshop at the college in Glasgow and almost immediately began to publish books himself. At first they were printed by other firms, but within a year Robert Foulis had his own press, and in 1743 was appointed the university's printer. For many years, the Foulis bookshop served as "a pleasant lounge and meeting place for students and others interested in books and literature," anticipating in a small way publisher and fellow-Scot John Murray's drawing room at 50 Albemarle Street in London (see p. 19). Though relatively small, the Foulis Press turned out almost 600 editions in the years between 1742 and 1776. Using quality paper and fine typefaces made locally by Alexander Wilson, an expert in the field, Robert and his brother Andrew, who had joined the firm toward the end of 1746, quickly established a Europe-wide reputation as "the Elzevirs of Britain" for their well-designed and immaculately executed editions of ancient classical texts, some printed in Greek alone, or Latin alone, some in Greek with a Latin translation, and some in English translation. In one of the rare studies devoted to the brothers and their press, it is claimed that the great German classicist Johann Joachim Winckelmann never traveled without Homer, "his companion at every instant of his life," and that the edition he had with him on his last journey (in the course of which he met his end) was that of Foulis, "very elegantly printed at Glasgow in 1756–58."[16]

Although a fair number of their books were produced specifically for collectors of select works and were printed on large and fine paper, vellum, linen, and satin, Robert's ideal printer was in fact not so much the Elzevirs as the great sixteenth-century French printer Robert Estienne, also known as "Robertus Stephanus." Thus the Foulis brothers also put out many relatively inexpensive "workman-like octavos and duodecimos" of both ancient and modern classics, as well as of the writings of professors at the college, such as Robert's mentor, the philosopher Francis Hutcheson, the social and political theorist John Millar, and the orientalist and natural scientist John Anderson (founder of Anderson's Institution, dedicated to natural science, and known, since 1964, as the University of Strathclyde). Although the Foulis's widely admired folio and quarto editions of the classics were expensive to produce and not always profitable—Robert's ideal of a folio edition of Plato, decades in preparation, was never realized—these manageable pocket-size volumes, intended for students and the general reader, were widely appreciated and were what kept the Press afloat financially, even though much effort was devoted to achieving high textual accuracy.[17] (The brothers employed a proofreader, which was not common practice at the time.[18]) The ancient classics were represented among the less elaborate volumes by editions, sometimes in the form of the author's complete works, of Aeschylus, Anacreon, Aristophanes, Aristotle, Caesar, Cicero, Cornelius Nepos, Demosthenes, Epictetus, Heliodorus, Herodotus, Homer, Horace, Juvenal, Longinus, Lucretius, Marcus Aurelius, Phaedrus, Pindar, Plato, Plautus, Pliny, Plutarch, Sappho, Sophocles, Tacitus, Terence, Theocritus, Theophrastus, Thucydides, Virgil, and Xenophon. The moderns included not only well-established classics,

such as Shakespeare, the fifteenth- to sixteenth-century Scottish poet William Dunbar, Milton, Thomas More, Dryden, Thomas Otway, and Locke, and relatively recent writers, such as Joseph Addison and Richard Steele, Congreve, John Gay of *The Beggar's Opera*, Pope, Matthew Prior, Nicholas Rowe, Shaftesbury, and John Vanbrugh, but also several contemporaries—Tobias Smollett, Samuel Johnson, Edward Young (of *Night Thoughts*), and Thomas Gray (of the celebrated *Elegy*). A deluxe quarto edition of Gray was even produced, which won general acclaim, not least from the author himself. "I rejoice to be in the hands of Mr. Foulis, who has the laudable ambition of surpassing his predecessors the *Etiennes* and *Elzevirs*," Gray declared.[19] In addition, the

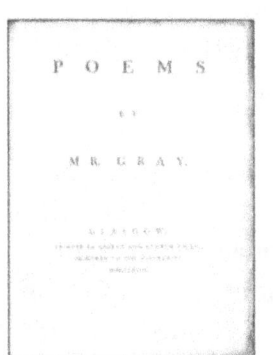

brothers published translations of Boileau, Bossuet, Cervantes, Fénelon, Le Sage, Tasso, and Voltaire. Their achievement, as described by Richard B. Sher and Andrew Hook, "was to translate into print culture the values of the classical, aesthetic, moralistic, Hutchesonian Enlightenment in Glasgow."[20]

Never a very large firm like Murray or Strahan or Constable, the Foulis Press shut down at the end of the century. Its financial status had become precarious even before it was taken over by

Robert's son Andrew, following the older Andrew's death in 1775 and that of Robert himself a year later. Increasing concentration on the popular duodecimo editions could not make up for the losses entailed by the firm's high-quality quartos and folios and Robert's longtime and passionate commitment, which he had pursued at great expense, to founding a local academy of art. Nevertheless, it had an impact on the culture of its time—and of the nineteenth and twentieth centuries—well beyond Glasgow or Scotland. Robert and Andrew Foulis, it has been said, were not only "the 'most important of the British classical publishers' in the eighteenth century, their pocket editions of English poets, begun in 1765, spawned a publishing phenomenon that has thrived from that day to this, from their own series to the Oxford World Classics." It is indeed ironic, in the words of the same scholar, "that printers such as Robert and Andrew Foulis, deeply imbued with the old-order ethos of a Robert Estienne, should have helped to pave the way for a mass market in poetry reprints, but that is what they did."[21]

John Murray (London) 1768

The great publishing house of Murray was founded in London in 1768 by Edinburgh-born John McMurray (1737–93), a former Royal Marines officer. Having acquired Willliam Sandby's London bookselling business at 32 Fleet Street in 1768, McMurray dropped the "wild highland Mac"[22] from his name, probably because of the then prevailing prejudice against the ever more numerous and ambitious Scots in the book trade. He soon built up a list of authors, including the Swiss poet, pastor, theologian, physician, philosopher, and physiognomist Johann Kaspar Lavater, and future Prime Minister Benjamin Disraeli's father, Isaac D'Israeli, whose popular *Curiosities of Literature* John Murray published in 1791 and with whose whole family both Murray Senior's family and that of his son and successor, John Murray II, maintained a long and close friendship. Both Murrays repeatedly sought and received advice from D'Israeli.[23] As for Lavater, the translation by Henry Hunter, minister of the Scots Church, London Wall, of his *Essays in Physiognomy* (1788–99)—a sumptuous volume containing hundreds of illustrations engraved by Thomas Holloway and William Blake—was John Murray I's financially most successful publication, making him a profit of around £1,000. Murray published many scientific and medical studies, as well as books in the developing fields we would now define as sociology and economics, such as Cesare Beccaria's *Discourse on Public Oeconomy and Commerce* (1769) and Glasgow professor John Millar's groundbreaking *Observations on the Distinction of Ranks in Society* (1771). In literature, he reprinted Lyttelton's *Dialogues of the Dead* of 1760 (1768 and 1774) and Walpole's *Castle of Otranto* of 1765 (1769); and published an abridged version of Hugh Blair's *Essays on Rhetoric* (1784), as well as translations of Marmontel's *Contes moraux* (1769) and of various tales by Voltaire (1774, 1776). In addition, he partnered with Strahan and Millar's successor, Thomas Cadell, in putting out editions of novels by Smollett, of Sterne's *Tristram Shandy* and *A Sentimental Journey* (both 1774), and a 10-volume edition of Sterne's *Complete Works* (1780). He also took shares in the sixth, corrected edition of Johnson's *Dictionary* (1778), a new nine-volume edition of the *Works of Henry Fielding* (1784), and Johnson's edition of *The Works of the English Poets* in 68 volumes (1779–81). In another field entirely, he was one of the founding sponsors of the London evening newspaper, *The Star*, in 1788.

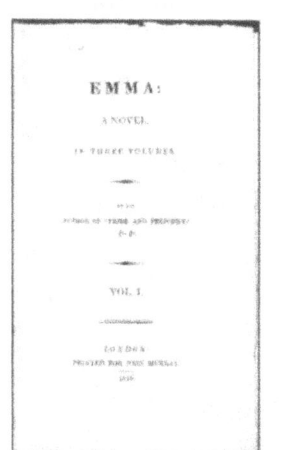

John Murray Senior was succeeded by his Edinburgh University-educated son, John Murray II (1778–1843), who made the house of Murray—in the words of another Scot, the great nineteenth-century liberal and progressive journalist Samuel Smiles, writing in 1873 —"a business destined to carry the name of John Murray wherever the English language was spoken, and wherever English books were read, as the most venturesome and yet the most successful publisher who has ever, in London at all events, encouraged the struggles of authorship and gratified the tastes of half a world of readers."[24] After Jane Austen's father failed to have her work accepted by Millar's successor, Thomas Cadell (in 1796 he declined *Pride and Prejudice*, then entitled *First Impressions*), and after the publisher Benjamin Crosby, having purchased the copyright of *Northanger Abbey* (then entitled *Susan*) in 1803 for £10, did nothing to publish the novel—the copyright of which Jane's brother bought back for her in 1816—Jane Austen finally succeeded in having *Sense and Sensibility* (completed in 1798 under the title *Elinor and Marianne*) published in 1811, *Pride and Prejudice* in 1813, and *Mansfield Park* in 1814 by London bookseller and publisher Thomas Egerton. In 1815, however, Austen moved her work to Murray, who put out *Emma* in 1815 and a second edition of *Mansfield Park* in 1816.[25]

Murray II was a close friend of many leading writers of the day, notably Walter Scott and Byron. He helped with the sale of Constable's editions of Scott, and Scott in turn was a regular contributor of articles and reviews to Murray's *Quarterly Review*, of which the third editor was John Gibson Lockhart, Scott's son-in-law and biographer, and, as already noted, a writer himself. In the case of Byron, Murray was the chief publisher of the phenomenally successful poet. *Childe Harold's Pilgrimage*, Byron's second book, which was put out by Murray on March 10, 1812, sold out in five days, whereas 10,000 copies of *The Corsair* were sold on the day of its publication in 1814—a remarkable figure by the standards of the day, when, because of the high price of paper, the similarly high cost of printing and production, and the limitations and uncertainty of the market, "the average edition of a serious book was around 750 copies," in the estimation of a modern scholar, and "only in very exceptional circumstances, such as Scott's novels, did editions in the early nineteenth century run to 6,000 copies."[26] Many other works by Byron followed, including the *Ode to Napoleon Buonaparte* in 1814. A 12-volume edition of the *Complete Works* appeared in 1814–24, and in 1826, Murray commissioned the popular poet Thomas Moore, a friend of his and of Byron's, to write Byron's biography. The first volume of *Letters & Journals of Lord Byron, with Notices of his Life*, published on January 1, 1830, was extremely well received, as was the second, which appeared eleven months later. Murray also commissioned Moore to prepare a new edition of Byron's *Complete Works*, and this was published in 1837. Having sought, after the great poet's death, to have Thorwaldsen's handsome statue of Byron placed in Westminster Abbey and been turned down by the dean, it was Murray who arranged for it to be moved from the warehouse where it had been stored and placed in the great library of Trinity College, Cambridge.

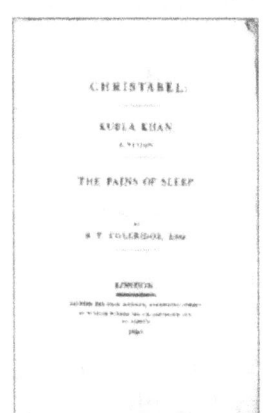

Thanks largely to Scott, Murray got to know, befriend, and publish—anonymously or under the pseudonym "Geoffrey Crayon, Gentleman"—the American writer Washington Irving (*Bracebridge Hall*, 1822, and *Tales of a Traveller*, 1824) and the poet George Crabbe (much admired in his own day by Austen, Scott, and Byron and in ours by T. S. Eliot). In addition, he maintained his father's close relationship with the D'Israeli family and published several works by Isaac, the elder D'Israeli—the collection of short stories entitled *Vaurien* (1797) and the second edition of *Romances* (1801; both in conjunction with T. Cadell); *Flim-Flams, or The Life and Errors of my Uncle and the Amours of my Aunt* (1805); *Despotism, or The Fall of the Jesuits: A Political Romance* (1811)—as well as the young Benjamin's novel *Contarini Fleming. A Psychological Auto-Biography* (4 vols., 1832), which "excited considerable sensation and was very popular at the time of its publication,"[27] and the almost 300-page-long pamphlet *England and France, or A Cure for the Ministerial Gallomania*, which the young Disraeli edited and to which he himself contributed substantially.[28] In 1813 Murray published a translation of Madame de Staël's *De l'Allemagne* and in 1814 he proposed to Coleridge, who, in 1800, had translated Schiller's *Piccolomini*, the first part of the *Wallenstein* trilogy, that he undertake a translation of Goethe's *Faust*. Unfortunately, this proposal did not work out. Murray's reputation as a publisher was such, however, that Coleridge (in 1814–15), Wordsworth (in 1826), and Carlyle (in 1831) all sought him out as a publisher of their works, though, for various reasons, with the exception of Coleridge's long gothic narrative poem *Christabel* (1816), none of their proposals was realized.[29]

The Murray drawing room at 50 Albemarle Street in Mayfair was "for some time the centre of literary friendship and intercommunication at the West End." The young George Ticknor from Boston described it in June 1815 as "a sort of literary lounge where authors resort to read newspapers and talk literary gossip." According to John Murray III, "it was in Murray's drawing-room that Walter Scott and Byron first met" and then "met there nearly every day." Other regular visitors included Southey, Mackenzie (of *The Man of Feeling*), the poets Crabbe and Coleridge, Washington Irving, and Madam de Staël (during her brilliant reception in England in 1813).[30] In 1809, with Scott's help, John Murray II launched the *Quarterly Review* as a Tory-inclined competitor to the already celebrated and highly successful Whig-inclined *Edinburgh Review*, which, as noted, was put out by fellow-Scot Archibald Constable (for many years a close friend and collaborator of Murray) in Edinburgh, and for which Murray himself had for a time been the London agent. Like its Edinburgh rival, The *Quarterly Review* did much to popularize literature in nineteenth-century Britain. It ceased publication only in 1967.

Unlike the Minerva Press or Thomas Norton Longman and partners, or even T. Cadell, with whom he often collaborated, or, for that matter, Edinburgh publishers Archibald Constable or William Blackwood, Murray seems to have been disinclined to publish contemporary novels, Jane Austen and Washington Irving being exceptions to what was probably a business as well as a cultural decision.[31] He did respond positively at first, in 1808—hence at an early point in his career—to a proposal, strongly supported by Scott, that he collaborate with Ballantyne of Edinburgh on a uniform edition of the "British Novelists," starting with Defoe and ending with the novelists of the close of the eighteenth century. This collection would have included works by 36 British and 18 foreign authors in English translation and would have had to be published in some 200 volumes. Despite pressure from the Ballantynes, Murray was apparently daunted by the financial risk involved, and backed out of the project.[32] A series, edited by Scott's son-in-law Lockhart and entitled "Murray's Family Library," was launched in 1829 but it lasted only until 1834 when, as it was running a deficit, it was sold to another publisher. Its fifty-one volumes included no works of fiction, only works of history and biography, such as Lockhart's own *Life of Napoleon Buonaparte,* Southey's *Life of Nelson*, Washington Irving's *Life and Voyages of Christopher Columbus*, Sir David Brewster's *Life of Sir Isaac Newton*, Sir John Barrow's *Life of Peter the Great*, Henry Hart Milman's *History of the Jews*, as well as a few reports of travel and exploration, such as John and Richard Lander's *Adventures in the Niger*, and an occasional work of natural history, such as *The Natural History of Insects*, edited by the Scottish physician Robert Ferguson. It was nonetheless a pioneering project; at 5/- per volume, it was less expensive than most similar publications at the time and in reaching out to a broader readership it anticipated the policies of other companies founded by Scots, such as Edinburgh-based Nelson and Glasgow-based Blackie, Collins, and Gowans and Gray.

In the mid-1820s, Murray began planning a daily newspaper, for which young Benjamin Disraeli provided the name—*The Representative*—and in the promotion and financing of which Disraeli was, at Murray's request, though still barely twenty years old, extraordinarily active. Disraeli invested his own funds in it, traveled to Scotland to persuade Walter Scott and his son-in-law John Gibson Lockhart that the latter should take on the editorship of it, and set up foreign correspondents for it all over Europe and the Middle East. The drastic failure of the paper barely six months after its launch on January 25, 1826, and Murray's loss thereby of about £27,000, caused a serious rift, albeit subsequently mended, between the two closely related Murray and D'Israeli families. Murray's own view was that he had "loved, not wisely, but too well" the young man of whom he had only shortly before, on September 25, 1825, written to Lockhart, by way of introduction, that he had "never met a young man of greater promise. He is a good scholar, hard student, a deep thinker, of great energy, equal perseverance, and indefatigable application. His knowledge of human nature, and the practical tendency of all his ideas, have often surprised me in a young man who has hardly passed his twentieth year."[33]

John Murray III (1808–92) continued the business and published Charles Eastlake's first English translation of Goethe's *Theory of Colours* (1840), David Livingstone's *Missionary Travels* (1857), and Charles Darwin's *Origin of Species* (1859). Murray III also contracted to publish Herman Melville's first two books, *Typee* (1846) and *Omoo* (1847) in England. Both were presented—in line with the Murrays' apparently considered standing back from the publication of novels—as nonfiction travel narratives. Both were included in a new series, "Murray's Colonial and Home Library," launched by John Murray III in 1843 in response to a new copyright law intended to protect British publishers in the colonies from cheap imports of pirated English-language works produced in the United States, France, and Belgium. Other books in the series, which ran until 1849, included Darwin's journals from his travels on the *Beagle*, George Borrow's *The Bible in Spain*, and Thomas Campbell's collection of *British Poets* (originally published by John Murray II in 1819). The prospectus of the new series articulates aims that had already inspired the short-lived "Murray's Family Library" of 1829–34 and, as noted, were to inspire other publishing enterprises founded by Scots. It deserves to be quoted at some length:

> The main object of this undertaking is to furnish the inhabitants of the Colonies of Great Britain with the highest Literature of the day, consisting partly of original Works, partly of new editions of popular Publications, at the lowest possible price. It is called for in consequence of the Acts which have recently passed the British Parliament for the protection of the rights of British authors and publishers, by the rigid and entire exclusion of foreign pirated editions. These Acts, if properly enforced, will, for the first time, direct into the right channel the demand of the Colonies for English Literature: a demand of which our authors and publishers have hitherto been deprived by the introduction of piracies from the United States, France, and Belgium. In order, therefore, that the highly intelligent and educated population of our Colonies may not suffer from the withdrawal of their accustomed supplies of books, and with a view to obviate the complaint, that a check might in consequence be raised to their intellectual advancement, Mr. Mur-

> ray has determined to publish a series of attractive and useful works, by approved authors, at a rate which shall place them within reach of the means not only of the Colonists, but also of a large portion of the less wealthy classes at home, who will thus benefit by the widening of the market for our literature.

John III's successor, John Murray IV (1851–1928), was publisher to Queen Victoria. He was responsible for the posthumous three-volume publication in 1907 of *The Letters of Queen Victoria*. He also put out *Murray's Magazine* from 1887 until 1891 and in 1917 he acquired the house of Smith, Elder & Co. (On this firm, see the entry that follows.) The house of Murray continued to be active under the direction of the Murray family until it was taken over by the Headline publishing group in 2002 and two years later by the French publisher Hachette.

John Bell (Edinburgh) 1771, Bell & Bradfute (Edinburgh) 1788

John Bell, the son of a minister, was apprenticed in 1754, aged eighteen, to the Edinburgh printer-publisher Alexander Kincaid and four years later was admitted to partnership with him, succeeding Alexander Donaldson, who set off on his own eventful career (see p. 4). The partnership with Kincaid was dissolved in 1771 when Kincaid joined up with another Scottish printer-publisher, William Creech, while John Bell set up in business on his own. The break may have been provoked by one of the copyright issues common at the time and briefly discussed previously (pp. 3–6). In business for himself, Bell continued the Scottish custom of printing and selling works still under copyright protection according to the London publishers and the Stationers' Company. Because of this, he became embroiled in a dispute with Thomas Cadell, the partner and successor of London Scot William Millar (who had already brought suit, on an earlier occasion, against Kincaid) and Cadell's associate, William Strahan (another London Scot who for several years had been urging Kincaid, his friend and former fellow-apprentice in Edinburgh, to break with Bell, over the publication of an alleged "pirated" edition of Ferguson's influential *Essay on the History of Civil Society*, originally published in 1767 by Millar and Cadell, in association with Kincaid and Bell as their agents in Edinburgh). Bell was certainly no stranger to so-called "pirated" editions. In 1774, three years after setting out on his own, he was sued in the Edinburgh Court of Session by the London bookseller and publisher James Dodsley for selling a "pirated" edition of Lord Chesterfield's *Letters to his Son* and a year later by Becket, Cadell, and Strahan for selling "pirated" editions of Sterne's *Works* and *A Sentimental Journey*. In 1781 he was once again pursued in court by Strahan and Cadell for marketing a "pirated edition" of John Gregory's best-selling *A Father's Legacy to his Daughters*, originally published by Cadell in 1774.

In 1785, however, Bell scored a coup when, in association with a giant of the London publishing and wholesale book trade, George Robinson[34] (a native of Dalston, near Carlisle in northwest England, close to the Scottish border, and a radical spirit, like Bell himself), he outbid Strahan and Cadell for the rights to Thomas Reid's *Essays on the Intellectual Powers of Man*, a basic text of the hugely influential "Scottish philosophy of common sense" that was to go through countless editions in the following decades.[35] In November 1788, Bell took his nephew and apprentice John Bradfute into the business as a partner and the new company of Bell & Bradfute soon made its mark as a prolific publisher of professional books on law, especially Scots law, but also, often in partnership with Robinson, in an expanding market for books in many fields of study—medicine, economics, mathematics, natural science, philosophy, history, travel and exploration, translations from Greek and Latin, grammars and instruction

manuals for the ancient and modern languages. The leading figures of the Scottish Enlightenment were well represented among the company's authors in the closing decades of the eighteenth century and the first half of the nineteenth by Ferguson, Hume, Kames, Monboddo, Playfair, Reid, William Smellie, Adam Smith, and Dugald Stewart.[36]

In literature, usually in association with other publishers, Bell & Bradfute brought out a number of established classics and favorites, beginning with *The Spectator, with Sketches of the Lives of the Authors and Explanatory Notes*, in eight volumes (1791, with further editions in 1793-94, 1802, and 1816) and soon afterward *The Works of William Shakespeare, in eight volumes, in which the beauties observed by Pope, Warburton, and Dodd are pointed out: together with the author's life, a glossary, copious indexes, and a list of the various readings* (1795). *A Complete Edition of The Poets of Great Britain, with the Lives of the Authors annexed, and with beautiful Vignettes* came out in 1792-95 in twelve octavo volumes. A *Life of Samuel Johnson,* published in 1795, was followed a decade later, in 1806—in collaboration with William Blackwood, Bell's former apprentice—by a fifteen-volume edition of *The Works of Samuel Johnson*, as well as a re-edition of Johnson's *Lives of the most eminent English Poets*. The one-volume anthology, *Gems from English Poets, Chaucer to Moore*, put out in 1842, may well have been intended to reach a relatively wide—if not yet popular—readership.[37] In the first half of the nineteenth century, Bell & Bradfute, which, after the death of Bell in 1806 and then of Bradfute, was run by a later partner, also republished—most often in association with one or more other publishers—fiction by Jane Austen (*Mansfield Park* [1833], *Northanger Abbey* [1833], *Pride and Prejudice* [1833], *Sense and Sensibility* [1833]), William Beckford (*Vathek* [1834]), Henry Fielding (*Tom Jones* [1805]), William Godwin (*Caleb Williams* [1832]), Mary Wollstonecraft Shelley (*Frankenstein or the Modern Prometheus* [1849]) and Tobias Smollett (*Peregrine Pickle*, with illustrations by Rowlandson [1805]). Among new literary works, frequently in association with the successful but for a time financially troubled London publisher R. Bentley, the firm put out, between 1832 and 1853, no fewer than twenty-six novels by the highly popular American writer James Fenimore Cooper; Washington Irving's *Tales of the Alhambra* (1835); several works by Bulwer-Lytton, including *Eugene Aram* (1836) and *The Last Days of Pompeii* (1839); and Maria Edgeworth's *Helen* (1838).

Foreign language and classical literatures, in many cases intended for use in schools, were not neglected: Caesar (multiple editions of *De Bello Gallico* between 1795 and 1839, *Opera Omnia* in 1832, 1838, 1873), Sallust (*Bellum Catalinae* and *Bellum Jugurthi-*

num before 1795 and in 1814, 1819, 1822, 1851), Cicero (*De Officiis* both in English translation, as *An Essay on Moral Duty* [1798], and in Latin [1812, 1819] and his *Orationes selectae* in 1802, 1807 and 1819, with an English translation in 1814, both together in Latin in 1812 and 1819), Tacitus ("editio nova ad usum scholarum") before 1795 and Cornelius Nepos (*Vitae excellentium imperatorum* in English translation as well as the original Latin [1794, 1812, 1825]). The *Iliad* in two duodecimo volumes was listed, in Greek with a Latin translation, in the firm's 1795 catalogue at a cost of 8 shillings and in further editions in 1809 and 1815, the *Odyssey* in 1810. Among modern foreign-language texts Fénélon's *Les Aventures de Télémaque* and Le Sage's *Gil Blas* were put out in the original French (1793 and 1799, respectively), whereas a translation of Rousseau's *La Nouvelle Héloïse* (*Julia, or The New Eloisa*) was issued in two duodecimo volumes, first by J. Bell in 1773 and then by Bell & Bradfute in 1794, to be followed by translations of Le Sage (*The Devil upon Two Sticks*) in 1774, of Mme de Genlis (*The Knights of the Swan, or The Court of Charlemagne*) in 1796, of Schiller (*The Robbers*) in 1800. The early decades of the nineteenth century saw the publication of Schiller's *Der Geisterseher*, translated as *The Ghost-Seer* (1831), Hugo's *The Hunchback of Notre Dame* (1833), Madame de Staël's *Corinne, or Italy* (1833), Manzoni's *The Betrothed* (1834), and Chateaubriand's *The Last of the Abencerages* (1835).

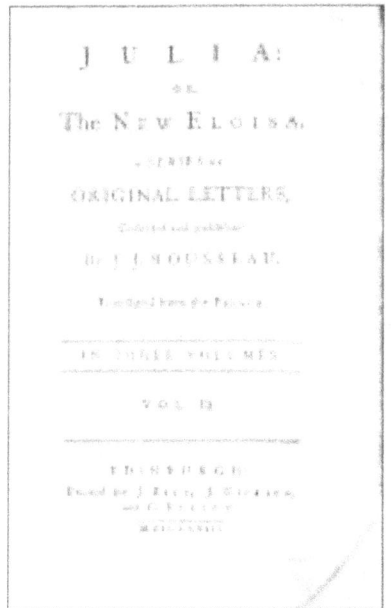

The prices of Bell & Bradfute's books are worth noting. Rousseau's *Julia or the New Eloisa* was for sale at three shillings for each of the two bound duodecimo volumes. Adam Ferguson's *Institutes of Moral Philosophy*, also duodecimo, was offered at three shillings and sixpence. Octavo volumes, such as Ferguson's *Essay on the History of Civil Society*, Hume's *Essays and Treatises*,

Reid's *Inquiry into the Human Mind: on the Philosophy of Common Sense*, or Smith's two-volume *Theory of Moral Sentiments*, sold for seven shillings a volume. Larger quarto volumes, such as Monboddo's *Of the Origin and Progress of Language* cost one pound. These prices seem somewhat lower than usual at the time.[38] It could well be, therefore, that in accordance with the Presbyterian Scots' conviction that instructive and improving literature should be widely available, Bell & Bradfute hoped to reach out to as broad a readership as possible.

Archibald Constable (Edinburgh) 1798

The son of a farmer in the eastern county of Fife, Archibald Constable—"the grand Napoleon of the realm of print," as Walter Scott dubbed him; "by far the greatest publisher Scotland has ever produced," according to Scott's son-in-law, John Gibson Lockhart[39]—developed an interest in books after visiting a local bookshop in the small Fife fishing port of Pittenweem. In 1788, his father arranged for him to be apprenticed to Peter Hill, an Edinburgh bookseller, and the fourteen-year-old gradually rose to a position of trust in the firm, being sent out to auctions with the power to make buying decisions. Hill was not especially interested in antiquarian books, but Constable was and, soon after his marriage in 1795, his father-in-law helped him set up his own business in the High Street in Edinburgh, specializing, as the sign above the shop read, in "Scarce Old Books."[40] The shop did well and in 1798 Constable ventured into publishing with a volume entitled *Fragments of Scottish History* by scholar and philosopher Sir John Graham Dalyell and a collection of *Doctrinal and Occasional Sermons* by the evangelically inclined preacher and theologian John Erskine (1721–1803), another native of Fife, who served as minister of Old Greyfriars Kirk in Edinburgh, along with historian and Principal of Edinburgh University William Robertson. In 1801 the young bookseller-publisher acquired the venerable *Scots Magazine*, the first volume of which had appeared in February 1739 (it recently claimed to be "the oldest magazine in the world still in publication in 2018"), and which regularly published wide-ranging articles and essays, reviews, poems, and current reports from all parts of the world. As its editor, he appointed the notable Scottish Orientalist John Leyden, who had a lively interest in Scottish poetry and was something of a poet himself. He also altered the title slightly to *The Scots Magazine and Edinburgh Literary Miscellany*.[41]

It was a year later, however, with the launching on October 10, 1802, of the *Edinburgh Review*—described by a recent scholar as "arguably the most politically, socially, and aesthetically significant periodical in British history"[42]—that the publishing house of Constable entered a new and significant phase of its history. The brainchild of the Reverend Sydney Smith ("smug Sidney," as Byron, after receiving a less than positive review in the *ER*, was to call him),[43] a 31-year-old, English-born Anglican curate with progressive ideas who had been sent to Edinburgh from his village in the South of England to supervise the studies at Edinburgh University of the local squire's son, the proposal for a new kind of journal devoted to substantive and wide-ranging book reviews by eminent experts was communicated in the late winter of 1801–02 to three of the Reverend's young Edinburgh-born friends. All three were advocates (i.e., in Scots law, barristers) with similar liberal and progressive ideas: 30-year-old Francis Jeffrey, who would later be Dean of the Faculty of Advocates; 23-year-old Henry Brougham ("blundering Brougham" according to Byron[44]), who would be appointed Lord Chancellor three decades later under the Whig government of Lord Grey; and 24-year-old Francis Horner, another strong Whig supporter, later elected several times to Parliament.[45] Together the four men approached Constable, who agreed to carry out their project. At first, no editor having been named, Smith acted in that capacity, to be succeeded, after he went back to England in 1803 by Jeffrey, who served as editor for almost three decades.

Eager to make the project succeed and appreciative of Jeffrey's literary skill and acumen, Constable heeded Smith's advice in the matter of the editor's salary and of payments to contributors. "If you will give £200 p.a. to your editor and ten guineas a sheet to contributors," Smith had told him, "you will soon have the best review in Europe."[46] The generous terms Constable offered reinforced his assurance to Jeffrey that, thanks to the adoption of an iron-clad rule requiring that all contributors be paid for their contributions, the new journal would be entirely independent of booksellers and publishers and he, Jeffrey, as editor, in full control of the selection process for the journal's content. The payments being generous, as Constable wished, the *Edinburgh Review* soon acquired distinguished contributors. In the first twenty-nine years or so, besides the four founders, they included Sir Walter Scott; the mathematician, geologist, and professor of natural philosophy at Edinburgh University John Playfair; the historian Henry Hallam; the poet Thomas Campbell; the political economist and demographer T. R. Malthus; the essayist William Hazlitt; Sir James Mackintosh, historian, professor of law and author of *Vindiciae Gallicae*, a celebrated defense of the French Revolution and critique of Burke; the enormously popular Presbyterian minister Thomas Chalmers, known for his concern with the living conditions of the poor; Francis Palgrave, founder of the Public Record Office and father of the celebrated anthologist; the great historian Thomas Babington Macaulay; the writer and critic Thomas Carlyle; and the Irish poet and friend of Byron and Shelley, Thomas Moore. Whereas previous review journals had usually been monthlies issued by booksellers and containing little more than summaries of books currently available for purchase, the new journal was distinguished by its careful selection of works for review rather than by their number, and by the

character of the reviews themselves as investigative and reflective essays of broad general interest and relevance inspired by the books under review (and most often, though not programmatically, liberally inclined), rather than simple presentations of their content.[47] The topics of the books reviewed ranged widely—history, political theory and political economy, mathematics and the natural sciences, as well as the literary, moral, and political implications of poetry, novels, plays, and essays. They thus appealed to cultivated and thoughtful readers not only in Scotland and Great Britain, but also throughout Europe.

There was indeed nothing provincial about Constable's *Edinburgh Review*, even though the many local Edinburgh discussion and debating clubs—among them the Poker Club, so named by Adam Ferguson and including Hume and Kames among its members; the Academy of Physicks, started by Brougham; and the Friday Club, started by Walter Scott—assuredly contributed to the *ER*'s roster of reviewers and to its general outlook and style.[48] Under the editorship of Jeffrey the *ER* addressed, as did the clubs, major figures and issues of European culture. Authors whose works were the occasion of review-articles in the first ten years (1802–12) include the Italian dramatist Vittorio Alfieri; the French Orientalist Anquetil-Duperron; Jeremy Bentham, the father of utilitarianism; the French scientist Claude-Louis Berthollet on questions of chemistry; Joseph Black, also on chemistry; Lord Byron; the poet Thomas Chatterton who fascinated the early Romantics because of his suicide in 1770 at the age of 17; the French paleontologist Georges Cuvier; the clergyman, surgeon, and poet George Crabbe whose realistic depictions of rural life impressed most of his fellow-poets; Joseph-Marie, Baron De Gerando on human knowledge; Vivant Denon on the celebrated 1798–1802 journey to and discovery of the art of Egypt; the novelist Maria Edgeworth; Ben Franklin, the great American scientist, statesman, inventor, and diplomat; the Anglo-Swiss painter Henry Fuseli or Füssli; the widely admired and influential German geographer, naturalist, and explorer Alexander von Humboldt; the Russian writer and historian Nikolai Karamzin; the German novelist, playwright, and rightwing diplomat August von Kotzebue and the liberal-minded German dramatist, critic, and philosopher Gottfried Ephraim Lessing; the Swedish botanist and taxonomer Carl Linnaeus; John Millar, the Glasgow professor of law, one of the founders of modern sociology; the budding novelist Amelia Opie; the pioneer economist David Ricardo; the hugely successful novelist and poet Walter Scott; the future Poet Laureate Robert Southey; and Germaine de Staël, the intimate friend of Benjamin Constant and August Schlegel, celebrated hostess of Coppet, and author of critical reflections on society and literature and of the novels *Delphine* (1802) and *Corinne* (1807), which explore the place of women in society and in the world of art and literature.

Seven hundred and fifty copies of the first number (October 10, 1802) were printed, selling at five shillings each. These were soon snapped up and a second edition of 750 copies was put out the following month. Within another year more than 2,000 copies of issue number 1 had been sold in Edinburgh alone.[49] "The most sanguine among us, even Smith himself," Brougham recalled later, "could not have foreseen the greatness of the first triumph."[50] By 1807, circulation of the journal, issued in four numbers annually, had risen to seven thousand, by the end of 1809 to eleven thousand, despite a modest increase in price, and by 1814 it had reached thirteen thousand. "No genteel family can pretend to be without it," Scott wrote in 1808, "because, independent of its politics [which, though not uniform, were on the whole not Scott's—L. G.], it gives the only valuable literary criticism that can be met with." Unfortunately, the drastic financial difficulties that beset the house of Constable in 1826 led to the *ER* being taken over by Longman, who had been the London agent for the journal and with whom Constable had often collaborated. Fortunately, however, the quality of the journal launched by Archibald Constable and sustained for a quarter of a century in Edinburgh was maintained and its influence in no way diminished, despite the arrival on the scene of several significant competitors. According to Mme de Staël, if someone came from another climate and desired "to know in what work the highest pitch of human intellect might be found, he ought to be shown *The Edinburgh Review*."[51]

In November 1805, Constable ventured into novel publishing with an anonymous work entitled *Belleville House*, co-published with a London and a Dublin firm; *The Mysterious Visitor, or Mary, the Rose of Cumberland* by Henry Montague Cecil, co-published with Longman of London; and *Adeline Mowbray, or The Mother and Daughter* by the prolific and widely read Mrs. Amelia Opie, also co-published with Longman. Throughout the years, although a great deal of his output consisted of writings on law, science, medicine, theology, and travel and exploration, Constable continued to publish fiction by popular writers of the time, including several women writers, or writers with a Scottish connection, often in association with Longman or, as of about 1820, Hurst, Robinson, another London publisher. Among them: William Godwin, *Mandeville. A Tale of the Seventeenth Century in England* (1817); Mary Brunton, *Emmeline* (1819, co-published with John Murray); Miss [M.G.T.] Crumpe, *Isabel St. Albe, or Vice and Virtue. A Novel* (1823). Perhaps because the novel was still regarded as a not quite respectable literary form, it was not uncommon at the time for novels to be published anonymously. Thus, Catherine Cuthbertson, author of *The Hut and the Castle* (1823), was identified only as "the author of 'The Romance of the Pyrenees'"; John Campbell Colquhoun's *Zoe: An Athenian Tale* (1824) appeared with no author's name; *Tales of the Wild and the Wonderful* (1825), an early work of George Borrow, who was to achieve fame later with *The Bible in Spain* [1843], *Lavengro* [1851], and *Romany Rye* [1857], also appeared with no author's name, though it did carry a dedication to the Scottish woman poet Joanna Baillie. *Reine Canziani: A Tale of Modern Greece* (1825) by a Glasgow-born poet, painter, and novelist, Catherine Grace Godwin, similarly carried no author's name. Three works by the successful novelist and playwright Charles Robert Maturin—*Woman, or Pour et Contre* (1818), *Melmoth The Wanderer* (1820, the work for which he is best known), and *The Albigenses: A Romance* (1824) were identified only as "by the author of . . ."

There is no question, however, that Constable's most significant and influential author was Sir Walter Scott. In 1802, Constable purchased a share in the third edition of Scott's *Minstrelsy of the Scottish Border* (1802) and partnered with Longman of London in the publication of Scott's edition of the thirteenth-century romance *Sir Tristrem* (1804) and again in that of Scott's first significant original success, *The Lay of the Last*

Minstrel (1805), which, within three years, had sold over 15,000 copies at the fairly high price of 25 shillings. In 1807 Constable offered Scott £1,000 in advance for his next major poem, *Marmion*, which went through four printings in the first year, amounting to 11,000 thousand copies, despite costing 31 shillings, and of which 50,000 copies had been sold by 1836). The following year, at Scott's urging, Constable published—this time in partnership with John Murray—*Quenhoo Hall: A Legendary Romance, being a History of Times Past*, by the recently deceased antiquary, engraver, and author Joseph Strutt (1749–1802). The title page described the work as "edited and partly written" by Scott, who also provided a preface for it. *The Lady of the Lake* appeared in 1810 and sold 20,300 copies in its first year at the steep price of 42 shillings.[52] In the wake of a critical review of Scott in the *Edinburgh Review*, a split occurred in 1808 between Constable and his most outstanding author, whereupon Scott transferred his business to the publishing firm of John Ballantyne & Co., for which he himself had supplied most of the capital and that was in fact his own venture into the publishing business. In 1813, however, a reconciliation took place between Scott and Constable. Ballantyne was in serious financial difficulties, and Scott approached Constable with a request to help out. As a result, Constable again became Scott's publisher, the condition being that Constable buy out the stock of the Ballantyne firm, which in turn was to be wound up at an early date. Scott was nevertheless to retain his interest in the printing business of James Ballantyne & Co.[53]

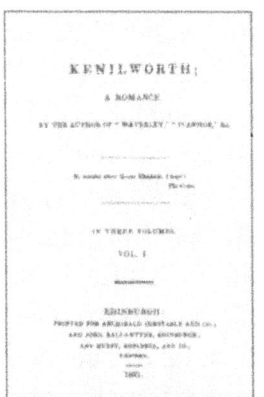

In the years that followed, Constable put out an impressive number of Scott's works. In 1814, following the renewal of their relationship, he bought the copyright of *Waverley*, Scott's first venture into prose fiction. At the author's insistence, it was issued anonymously;[54] but in a short time 12,000 copies had been sold. Scott's other novels followed in quick succession and all sold well: *Guy Mannering* in 1815; *The Antiquary* in 1816; *Rob Roy* in 1818; *The Abbot, Ivanhoe,* and *The Monastery* in 1820; *Kenilworth* in 1821; *The Fortunes of Nigel, Peveril of the Peak,* and *The Pirate* in 1822; *Quentin Durward* in 1823; *Redgauntlet* and *St. Ronan's Well* in 1824; *Tales of the Crusaders* in 1825; and *Woodstock, or The Cavalier. A tale of the Year Sixteen Hundred and Fifty-One* in 1826.

In 1812, Constable, at the height of success, despite the temporary defection of Scott, purchased the copyright of the *Encyclopædia Britannica*, and added a significant supplement of six volumes (1816–24) to the fourth, fifth and sixth editions. As part of his 1813 deal with Scott, Constable also took over the *Edinburgh Annual Register*, along with the Ballantyne company's stock of unsold copies of that massive publication, which had been Scott's idea and which had almost certainly contributed to John Ballantyne's financial problems. (Launched in 1808, it was losing £1,000 a year by 1812.[55]) The first volume to appear under the Constable name—for the year 1814—came out in 1816. It was a bulky volume of over 400 pages. Part 2 of the volume contained poems by Byron ("The Guerilla"), Wordsworth ("The Stranger"), Coleridge ("Isabelle"), Southey ("Peter of Barnet"), James Hogg ("Prayer of a Dying Soldier on the Field of Waterloo") and three unsigned sonnets, along with twenty-seven closely printed pages of bibliography for the year, arranged by subject matter and including substantial sections on "Novels and Romances" and "Poetry" (one of the longest), alongside sections on botany, chemistry, history, hydrology, law, mathematics, mechanics, medicine (including anatomy and surgery), philology, philosophy, political economy, theology, topography, and more.[56]

This work proved as big a burden to Constable, even after a drastic reduction in the number of copies printed, as it in all likelihood had been to Ballantyne since its first launch. Excessive speculation added to the firm's financial difficulties, and in 1826 when there was a general financial crash, Constable's London agents stopped payment, and the firm failed for over £250,000, while the printing business of James Ballantyne & Co. also went bankrupt for over £90,000. Sir Walter Scott, having contracted all of Ballantyne's bills, was affected by the failure of both firms, so that he, too, went bankrupt for over £126,000. To add insult to injury, Constable learned that Scott would thenceforth publish with another publisher. As already noted, publication of the *Edinburgh Review* was taken over by Longman.

Another casualty of the Constable firm's financial collapse was a projected *Elementary Encyclopedia.* In August 1823, Constable had informed Maria Edgeworth, the influential novelist and author of children's books, with whom, thanks to Scott, he entertained friendly relations and a correspondence, of his plans for an "Elementary Encyclopaedia for Youth." He had also discussed the project with her during a visit she had made to Scotland and had sounded her out about becoming one of the project's editors. Toward the end of 1824 he had sent her a printed list of the proposed contents, along with a request that she contribute articles on "Female education," "Etiquette," and "Recreations—Rational and Useful for the Female Sex." In her response of a few weeks later, Edgeworth greeted the proposal positively, while offering some suggestions for making the projected work more useful and accessible to its intended readership of the young or less educated. "In referring to an encyclopaedic dictionary, young people especially want immediate and precise information of the meaning of certain terms, or of the means of accomplishing certain purposes. It should be therefore more practical than theoretic. If I were you, in the first place I would weed out all the heads in your present prospectus which would be general treatises, and class the others into what are essential, necessary in the next degree, and so on. When you have thus got rid of what is obviously superfluous for your purpose, compress again and again till you get your design into the smallest compass that will hold the needful."[57] The encyclopedia, which Constable had hoped would begin production in May 1825, with all four volumes out by 1827, never materialized.

Constable's ambitious, pioneering plan for a series of mass-produced, cloth-bound books to be known as *Constable's Miscellany* was also a near-casualty of the company's fall into bankruptcy. Costing "a half a crown" or even one shilling each, the

Miscellany was to make "Original and Selected Publications in the various Departments of Literature, Science, and the Arts" available to the less well-off members of society and thus to "sell, not by thousands or tens of thousands, but by hundreds of thousand—ay, by millions!" Or, as announced with less panache on the first page of the first volume, with its dedication to King George IV, "This Miscellany" is "designed to extend useful Knowledge and elegant Literature by placing Works of Standard Merit within the attainment of every Class of Readers." Constable's preface to the first volume, dated Edinburgh, December 1825, expanded on this theme. The entire project—"one of the most significant publishing breakthroughs of the nineteenth century," in the words of the historian D. A. Low[58]—was clearly inspired by the characteristic Scottish emphasis on education and the dissemination of knowledge and culture (as, also, no doubt, by the no less characteristic Scottish business sense and interest in turning a profit).

> The change that has gradually taken place during the last thirty or forty years in the numbers and circumstances of the reading public, and the unlimited desire of knowledge that now pervades every class of society, have suggested the present undertaking. Previously to the commencement of the late war, the buyers of books consisted principally of the richer classes—of those who were brought up to some of the learned professions, or who had received a liberal education. The saving of a few shillings on the price of a volume was not an object of much importance to such persons, many of whom prized it chiefly for the fineness of its paper, the beauty of its typography, and the amplitude of the margins—qualities which add to the expense of a work, without rendering it in any degree more useful. But now, when the more general diffusion of education and of wealth has occasioned a vast increase in the number of readers and in the works which daily issue from the press, a change in the mode of publishing seems to be called for. The strong desire entertained by most of those who are engaged in the various details of agriculture, manufactures, and commerce, for the acquisition of useful knowledge and the cultivation of their minds is strikingly evinced by the establishment of subscription libraries and scientific institutions, even in the most inconsiderable towns and villages throughout the empire.

The Miscellany did get off the ground, but it was not without difficulty or delay. In 1825, Constable traveled to London to seek financial support for his project but banker after banker showed him the door. He returned to Edinburgh and fell ill with dropsy (edema). Another trip to London in January 1826 was equally futile, and in the middle of that month it became known that Constable and Company could not meet its obligations. Though it had been strongly endorsed by Walter Scott, the projected Miscellany could not count on material support from the great writer, whose financial situation was also dire. The naval captain and explorer Basil Hall, one of the Constable firm's authors (*Account of a Voyage of Discovery to the West Coast of Corea and the Great Loo-Choo Island in the Japan Sea*, 1818), who had been scheduled to contribute an early volume to the Miscellany, generously offered to donate his manuscript. Replying on May 29, 1826, to Hall's gesture, Constable was still not confident that his project would survive: "I cannot positively say that the arrangement for the Miscellany with my trustees will be completed within a week, though I hope it may be so."[59] Constable did succeed in getting the publication started, just before his death (in his early fifties) in July 1827. The first volume (1826) was a reprint, revised and enlarged, of Hall's 1818 *Account of a Voyage of Discovery to the West Coast of Corea*. Another work by Hall, in two volumes (*Extracts from a Journal Written on the Coasts of Chile, Peru, and Mexico in the Years 1820, 1821, 1822*), made up volumes II and III of the *Miscellany*. After Archibald Constable's death, the project was continued by his son Thomas, who took over the firm. In conformity with Constable's plans for the collection, most volumes were devoted to "practical" topics (history, geography, engineering, travel accounts, etc.). Early texts of a somewhat more literary character include a reprint of the *Memoirs of the Marchioness de la Rochejacquelin*, edited with a preface by Sir Walter Scott (vol. V, 1827); Lockhart's *Life of Burns* (vol. XXIII, 1828); Robert Chambers's two-volume *History of the Rebellions in Scotland in 1745–1746* (vols. XV, XVI, 1827); followed by Friedrich Schiller's *History of the Thirty Years' War* (vols. XVIII and XIX, 1828); Chambers's

History of the Rebellions in Scotland, under Montrose and Others, from 1638 till 1660 (vols. XXXI and XXXII, 1828) and *History of the Rebellions in Scotland under the Viscount of Dundee and the Earl of Mar in 1689 and 1715* (vol. XLII, 1829).[60]

In 1839, just over a decade after Archibald Constable's death, the author of a *Dictionary of Printers and Printing*, paid tribute to him. "A man joining such professional abilities to such liberal and extensive views; so capable of appreciating literary merit, and so anxious to find for it employment and reward; as largely endowed with the discernment, tact, and manners, necessary to maintain a useful, honourable, and harmonious intercourse with literary men, is not a common character, even among the improved race of modern bibliopolists."[61]

The business of the Constable firm was carried on by the publisher's son Thomas, who also took over and expanded the Edinburgh printing business of his grandfather, David Willison (Archibald Constable's father-in-law). In 1839 Thomas was appointed printer to Queen Victoria and in 1859 printer to Edinburgh University. By 1852 the company had sixteen presses and fonts for printing in Greek, Hebrew, Arabic, Sanskrit and German, as well as for printing music. As printer, T. Constable produced books for several major London publishing houses. He did not abandon publishing, however. As noted, volumes for the Miscellany continued to appear, along with other new works—under the name T. Constable, Edinburgh—primarily in history, philosophy, science, and religion, such as Alexander Wilson's *American Ornithology* (1831) and Dugald Stewart's *Collected Works* in 11 volumes (1854–60). After Thomas sold out his stock in 1860 to devote himself to writing, his son Archibald formed a new publishing company, which identified itself until about 1890 as "T. & A. Constable." By 1891, ten years after Thomas's death, the firm had relocated to London and presented itself on the title pages of the books it published as "Westminster: A. Constable" or "Westminster: Archibald Constable and Co." The new firm continued along the path followed by Thomas Constable, but was more active than the latter had been in recruiting contemporary poets, dramatists, novelists, and artists. Among the books published by A. Constable and Co.: George Meredith's *The Amazing Marriage*

(1895), Alice Meynell's *London Impressions* (1898), George Bernard Shaw's *Man and Superman* (1903) and *The Doctor's Dilemma* (1911), George Gissing's *The Private Papers of Henry Ryecroft* (1903), the poet Laurence Binyon's verse play *Paris and Oenone* (1906), Arthur Symons's *William Blake* (1907), Hilaire Belloc's *On Anything* (1910), and *Through China with a Camera, with over 100 illustrations* by the celebrated Scottish photographer John Thomson (1898), not to mention Bram Stoker's *Dracula* (1897). Set up in 1910, the once again renamed firm of "Constable and Co." published the popular poet Walter De la Mare's *A Child's Day* and *The Listeners and other poems* (1912), followed by *Peacock Pie* (1913) and four other books of poems; Katherine Mansfield's *The Garden Party and other stories* (1922), along with additional collections of her short stories and two volumes of her poems (1923 and 1924); and essays by the provocative writer on sexuality, Havelock Ellis (*Impressions and Comments* [1921], *The Dance of Life* [1923]). The close Scottish connection of the great publishing firm had by then been severed, however. In Edinburgh, Constable survived only as a printer.

Thomas Nelson (Edinburgh) 1798

Born in 1780 near Bannockburn—the Stirlingshire site of a celebrated victory of the Scots under Robert the Bruce over Edward II of England in 1314—Thomas Neilson left his family's farm in 1796 and, after several forays into different forms of employment, undertook an apprenticeship at a bookseller's in London. Two years later, on returning to Scotland, he founded the company that bears his name (slightly modified in 1818 in response to a potential misspelling on cheques) as a modest second-hand bookshop at 2 West Bow, just off the Grassmarket in Edinburgh. In view of the demand for used books that his bookselling business allowed him to observe, Nelson calculated that there was a market for cheap editions of standard works and, as he was of strict Covenanter stock,[62] began publishing religious texts in monthly "parts"—so-called "number-publications"[63]—such as Bunyan's *Pilgrim's Progress* (1678) in 1801, and John Howie's *Biographia*

Scoticana or Scots Worthies (1775) in 1812. From the outset, the emphasis was on price, the goal to put significant—and edifying—writings within reach of a broader than usual public, one that included an expanding skilled working class and, increasingly, the young. Inevitably most of Nelson's publications were reprints. Robertson's *History of Scotland during the Reigns of Queen Mary and King James VI* was put out in 1820; Smith's *Wealth of Nations, with a Life of the Author; also a View of the Doctrine of Smith* in 1827, with many subsequent reprintings between that date and midcentury; *The Works of Robert Burns* in 1831; Goldsmith's *History of the Earth and Animated Nature* in 1831 and *The Vicar of Wakefield* in 1839. Defoe's *Robinson Crusoe* appeared in 1835 or 1836 in an illustrated adaptation specially designed—already—for juvenile readers. To achieve his goal, Nelson employed new techniques of production and distribution. The company was one of the first to use stereotyping for large print runs at the press that it set up at Hope Park in Edinburgh in 1845, and in 1850 one of Thomas Nelson's sons, also named Thomas, came up with an important new invention, the rotary press, which, like the stereotype, reduced the cost of large print runs. In response to the hostility of booksellers dismayed by the low prices of his books and thus of the profit to be made from selling them, Thomas Nelson, Sr. resorted to direct sales at fairs and markets and to auctions in vacant stores rented for the purpose.[64] On the basis of his own experience as "a bagman with religious proclivities," during his London bookseller's apprenticeship, and of his considerable success at that time in obtaining subscriptions for works, such as the Stratford edition of Henry's Bible, which was sold in shilling parts, he in turn employed a "bagman," or traveling salesman, to hawk his products around Scotland and the North of England and to find outlets in small towns. He also soon expanded the range of his publications to include more classics, such as Thomson's *Seasons* (1840) or William Cowper's *Poems* (1842). "He was a pioneer in the production of literature for the million," according to the biographer, writing in 1889, of William Nelson, another son of Thomas Nelson, Senior, "but he catered for the taste of an age very different from our own, in his effort to put standard works, already stamped with the approval of the wise and good, within reach of the peasant and the artisan."[65]

In other words, Thomas Nelson was not actively promoting new literature; his business was with established, above all morally sound, and "improving" texts, or with new works that would contribute to the morals and the education of the young or uneducated. As the author of the article on him in the *Dictionary of Literary Biography* put it, he was moved by an "urge to spread learning and knowledge through good cheap books across a wider section of the population than had previously enjoyed it. This is the evangelism of the educator, of the democrat who wishes to see all people participating in the community of the learned." It did not hurt that, smartly pursued, it was also a highly profitable activity, or that it might help to quiet restlessness in the new working class, to promote a sense of a common culture, a national literature, across class and income boundaries, and to protect literature itself from the threat posed by cheap, mass-produced popular fiction.[66]

After sons William and Thomas, Jr. became—in 1835 and 1839, respectively—partners in the firm (renamed "Thomas Nelson and Sons" in 1858) and effectively took over the running of it, their father having become a virtual invalid in the twenty years before his death in 1861, the business continued along the lines set out at the start, but also expanded into new territories. In 1844 a London branch was opened by Thomas Nelson, Jr. in the very street, Paternoster Row, where his father had served his apprenticeship. A decade later an American branch was established in New York—the first branch of a British publishing house to be set up in the United States. As trade with the Empire, especially in the area of educational publications, became a more and more significant part of the firm's activities, offices were opened in Toronto, Cape Town, and Melbourne. The production side of the business also expanded. From 1839, when Thomas Nelson, Jr. joined the firm, most, if not all, of Nelson's printing was done in-house, at a facility in Castlehill; subsequently, as of 1845, as the company began to publish more and more original works, as well as reprints, at a larger, ever-expanding factory at

Hope Park, and finally after a major fire in 1878 destroyed those premises, causing over £100,000 worth of damage, printing was done at a vast and imposing newly built factory at Parkside just below the notable Edinburgh landmark of Arthur's Seat. (The Parkside works survived until 1968 when they were razed to make room for the premises of a large insurance company.)

With the opening of the Hope Park works, Nelson extended the range of the firm's publications to include contemporary fiction, history, and, above all books designed specifically for young audiences and for schools. Among fictional texts for adults, translations of foreign works, such as Dumas's *The Black Tulip* and *The Queen's Necklace* (both 1850), Hugo's *Toilers of the Sea* (1866) and *Les Misérables* (1870s), figured prominently alongside reprints of George Eliot and Dickens and the earliest publication in Britain of works by the American writer Nathaniel Hawthorne. That there was keen attention to commercial considerations is indicated by an unusual number of translations of the best-selling historical novels and semifictional biographies of the prolific (now virtually forgotten) mid-nineteenth-century German writer Luise Mühlbach: *The Merchant of Berlin. An Historical Romance* (1866); *Berlin and Sans Souci, or Frederick the Great and his Friends* (1867); *Louisa of Prussia and her Times: A Historical Novel* (1867); *Henry VIII and his Court, or Catherine Parr: A Historical Novel* (1867); *The Empress Josephine* (1867); and *Queen Hortense* (1870).[67] The firm's early emphasis on books for the young and on cheap but well-produced editions of the English-language classics for the ever-expanding upper working and lower middle classes was maintained, however. Along with their Glasgow counterparts, Collins and Blackie, the Nelson firm was thus set to become one of the pioneer developers of a vast new market for works of literature.

First, books for the young. According to a historian of Victorian children's literature, the publishing of religiously inspired fiction for the young was "the foundation of [Nelson's] commercial success."[68] School societies and, later, school boards listed Nelson titles among those suggested as suitable prize or reward books. R. M. Ballantyne's *Snowflakes and Sunbeams, or, The Young Fur Traders* (1856) was among the earliest books specially written for young people and published by Nelson. William Nelson himself suggested to the author—a nephew, as it happens, of the James Ballantyne who had been Sir Walter Scott's printer—that he draw on his experiences while serving, from age 16 to age 21 (1841–47), as a clerk of the Hudson's Bay Company on remote Canadian trading stations to write a story suitable for young readers. Ballantyne had literary ambitions. He had already published *Hudson's Bay, or Everyday Life in the Wilds of North America*, privately at first, for friends, family, and subscribers, then, in the same year, with Blackwood, who had been one of the subscribers to the privately produced book. In 1853 he had brought out *The Northern Coasts of America and the Hudson's Bay Territories: A Narrative of Discovery and Adventure* (a revised and expanded version of a work by an earlier author, first publishedi n 1832). He accepted Nelson's proposal with alacrity. There was never any doubt that whatever he came up with would meet the evangelically inclined Nelsons' strict requirement of high moral standards, for Ballantyne was himself a deeply religious man who believed he had a mission to employ his ability to write for young people under "guidance from God."[69] Over a dozen best-selling books for the young followed the 1853 volume, among them *Ungava: A Tale of Esquimaux Land* (1858) and *The Coral Island: A Tale of the Pacific Ocean* (also 1858)—a work that influenced Robert Louis Stevenson's writing of *Treasure Island* (1883) and that was still being read by young people in the twentieth century

(the present writer included).[70] Ballantyne's contribution to Nelson's list of books for boys was supplemented a couple of decades later by another dozen or so tales of adventure by the no-less-prolific and popular W. H. G. Kingston, with titles such as *Twice Lost: A Story of Shipwreck and of Adventure in the Wilds of Australia* (1876); *The Wanderers, or Adventures in the Wilds of Trinidad and up the Orinoco* (1897); and *On the Banks of the Amazon, or A Boy's Journal of his Adventures in the Tropical Wilds of South America* (1901). All these works went through several editions. As the editor of a more recent edition of *The Coral*

Island points out, "the romantic adventure-story in which the hero roams the world, making discoveries, doing good, but never overtly seeking wealth had become one of the main genres of popular fiction; and it had become enmeshed with imperial ideology, contributing to the national perception of the might and the right of the British Empire and suppressing awareness of its rapacious mercenary base."[71]

Nelson also engaged in publishing fiction for girls, the corresponding goal of which was not only to develop their reading skills but to teach them to be modest, Christian, chaste, charitable, and dedicated to their families. One of the chief suppliers of fiction for girls was the extraordinarily productive Charlotte Maria Tucker (who signed herself ALOE—A lady of England). Nelson published over thirty novels or collections of tales by her with titles such as *Stories Illustrating the Proverbs* (1858); *The Young Pilgrims: A Tale Illustrative of 'The Pilgrim's Progress'* (1859); *The Thorn in the Conscience and Other Stories* (1875); *The Silver Casket, or The World and its Wiles* (1877); *Stories from Jewish History* (1880). Catherine D. Bell was another Nelson author of juvenile books. Again the titles make clear their edifying and moralizing character: *Kind Words to Domestic Servants* (1857); *The Children's Mirror, or What is my Likeness?* (1859); *Mind Your Own Business* (1861); *Love Thy Neighbour as Thyself, or The Story of Mike, the Irish Boy* (1861); *The Way to be Happy, or The Story of Willie, the Gardener Boy* (1872).

In addition, for the very young, Nelson published simple texts, such as *Short Stories in Words of One or Two Syllables* (1869), as well as a periodical for juveniles: *The Children's Paper.* (Launched in 1855, it had a monthly circulation in 1880 of 30,000 and lasted until 1925.) The aim and impact of Victorian books for the young, including the many put out by Nelson, has been summarized by a modern critic: "By the fourth decade of the century the stories began to carry a social as well as a religious message. Not only were the young to be convinced of innate sinfulness, they were also to be socialized into prescribed roles, partly to maintain the status quo in a society which was undergoing, most uneasily, a radical transformation." In the literature for boys, "evangelicism gave way to imperialism, as the exigencies of spiritual bliss or woe became gradually more extraneous to the task of maintaining the Empire. [...] Books for girls, on the other hand, were generally content with reinforcing simple old-fashioned moral and social codes, and with justifying and inculcating unpalatable social roles."[72]

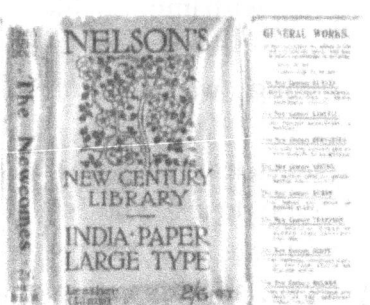

Truly talented new authors seem not to have been attracted by or to Nelson as a publisher. In a note to a partner of the firm toward the end of the century, one individual, under consideration as a possible editor of a projected boys' magazine, observed that the Nelson list included few or no "first class" contemporary novelists and that there was "an undoubted prejudice on the part of writers in the first rank towards your House. Right or wrong, just or unjust, it exists to a larger extent than I supposed."[73] The reasons for this may well have been partly a reputation for parsimony in its dealings with authors (such as led to Ballantyne's finally moving to Routledge), and partly the very image of the imprint. The one modern writer who enjoyed something of a reputation, even if he is hardly now considered to be "in the first rank"—namely, John Buchan—had in fact joined the firm in late 1906 as literary adviser and head of its London office, thanks to a close personal friendship that he and Thomas Arthur Nelson had formed as students at Oxford. Though Buchan did succeed in winning some original and creative modern writers for the firm's lists (William James, Joseph Conrad, H. G. Wells), Nelson's contribution to English literature must be seen chiefly in the form of the firm's spectacular success at making established classics available to readers of limited means in decently produced volumes at modest prices.

The first of the many series put out by Nelson in response to the Education Acts of 1870 (England) and 1872 (Scotland) was the Royal Readers. Though they made use of a broad range of short stories and poems, these were not literary texts but school "readers" intended to promote comprehension, proper diction, and literacy in general. They were used throughout the English-speaking world and were enormously successful—and profitable, contributing substantially to the financial health of the company.[74] (There were even, especially at a later stage, in the mid-twentieth century, but as early as 1887, versions in some of the languages of Africa.[75]) Almost inevitably, the Royal Readers also functioned as instruments of imperial ideology.[76] Of greater significance from the point of view of literary history were the many series of inexpensive but quite handsomely produced literary texts that the company put out in vast numbers. Among them, the New Century Library was started in 1899, and by 1904 offered twenty-five classic titles by Sir Walter Scott, thirteen by Dickens, fourteen volumes of the complete works of Thackeray, a two-volume set of Jane Austen, along with works by Charlotte Brontë, Bunyan, Burns, Carlyle, Cervantes, Washington Irving, Charles Kingsley, Bulwer-Lytton, and Tennyson, all clearly printed on good-quality paper and bound in cloth or leather, at two shillings and sixpence, or, in the United States, through the American branch of the company in New York, at $1.00, $1.50, or $2.00, "according to style of binding" but in all cases "superbly bound in cloth and various artistic leathers, limp, and board," in the words of a company advertisement in *The School Journal* for June 24, 1905. The Sixpenny Classics series, launched in 1903 (renamed simply "Nelson Classics" soon after) and claiming to offer "the best and cheapest books in the world," consisted by 1914 of 123 titles by fifty-four well-established classic authors—including Balzac, Darwin, Dickens, Benjamin Disraeli, Longfellow, Thackeray, Tolstoy, and Trollope—with twenty-one more titles announced for 1914. Eventually this series was made up of 400 works, mostly classics of English literature, but with a not insignificant number of foreign works among them, notably works by Dumas and Hugo. The Nelson Library of books selling for sevenpence dates from 1907 and again included major English classics and some foreign-language classics.

In 1910, Nelson and Sons branched out to Paris and began publishing cheap editions of French classics in French for the French market. Printed and bound in Edinburgh to the same high material standards as the firm's series of English classics, these sold in large quantities in France. They included, along with a set of the Complete Works of Victor Hugo, the French classical authors of the seventeenth century—Corneille, Molière, Racine, Mme de Sévigné, and La Bruyère—together with great eighteenth- and nineteenth-century authors, such as Rousseau, Mme de Staël, Chateaubriand, Vigny, George Sand, Balzac, and Flaubert, and a number of twentieth-century writers—Maurice Barrès, René Bazin, Pierre Loti, and Maurice Maeterlinck. Some of the great Russian novelists were also featured in French translation. The present writer's copy of Emile Zola's *Une Page d'amour*, published in the Collection Nelson in 1931, lists 160 works in the Collection—some by quite modern, or even contemporary writers, such as Henry Bordeaux and Georges Duhamel.[77] The French branch of the company, it could even be said, was more open to contemporary writers, albeit not the most challenging of them, than the British branch.

The contribution of Thomas Nelson and Sons, in sum, was not, like that of Murray or Strahan or Smith and Elder or Blackwood, to have promoted contemporary literary creation, unless quite indirectly through the company's educational program. It was to have made the great, already well-established classics of English literature, including those of the nineteenth century, accessible and familiar to a vast popular readership—an undertaking that had been greatly facilitated by the 1842 Copyright Act, which repealed former Copyright Acts, set clear limits to a book's copyright (either the life of the author and seven years after his death, or forty-two years from the date of publication, whichever was the longer), and protected the British and colonial markets from the import of books first published in Britain but reprinted outside the British dominions (chiefly in the United States).[78]

John Ballantyne (Edinburgh) 1808

About the firm of John Ballantyne & Co. there is not much to say. It is listed here chiefly because of its links to Walter Scott and Constable.

John Ballantyne (1774–1821) was the younger brother of James Ballantyne, for a time the printer of Walter Scott's works, and was first employed in his brother's printing establishment.

In 1808, in the wake of a dispute with Constable, his regular publisher until then, over a severely critical review of his work in *The Edinburgh Review*, Walter Scott essentially set up a publishing firm of his own, under the name of John Ballantyne & Co., with John Ballantyne as its manager. One of the first works produced by the new company was the *Edinburgh Annual Register*, intended by Scott to be not only a competitor and rival of the *Annual Register*—founded in 1758 under the editorship of Edmund Burke and offering records and copious analyses of the year's major events, developments, and trends throughout the world—but in some measure a conservative, Tory-inclined alternative to the liberal, Whiggish *Edinburgh Review* being put out by Constable. Scott had in fact first invited Constable to undertake publication of the new periodical and then excluded him from participation in it in response to Constable's cautious and skeptical view of the proposal and in the wake of the two men's falling out over the criticism of Scott in the *Edinburgh Review*. The first volume, for the year 1808, appeared in 1810, and was largely overseen by Scott and Robert Southey, the latter being charged with the extensive historical sections or chapters. It is an impressive compilation in two parts, the first consisting of 459 pages devoted to the "History" of Europe in the year 1808, followed by a further 103 pages of "State Papers." The second consisting of 240 pages devoted to a "Chronicle" of the year's events, followed by a further 200 pages, a few devoted to prices of stocks and bonds; statistics of deaths from diseases; and notable births, marriages, and deaths; and far longer sections devoted to "The Drama" (seventy-two pages); "The Fine Arts" (sixteen pages); changes to the laws (thirty-one pages); "The Physical Sciences" (forty-four pages); "The Living Poets of Great Britain" (written by Scott himself, twenty-seven pages); original poetry by the Scottish woman poet Joanna Baillie, Scott, Southey, and several less well-known poets; and a few anonymous pieces (forty-eight pages). The work closed on a thirty-two page bibliography of "New Publications for 1808" arranged by topic ("Antiquities," "Agriculture," "Architecture," "Arts and Sciences," "Biography," "Botany," etc.), and including substantial sections on "Drama," with twenty-five items listed; "Novels and Romances," with seventy-seven items listed, a fair number of them either in French or translated from the French of Mme de Genlis and Mme Cottin; and "Poetry," with about seventy items listed, including a few in foreign languages.

As described by a modern scholar,

> Southey's contributions [to the *Annual Register*] brought mixed reviews—expressions of disgust from Byron and Shelley, annoyance from Wordsworth, high praise from Coleridge ("the noblest specimen of recent and progressive History in the annals of Literature")—and a substantial income [of £400 a year], as well as the basis for much of his later *History of the Peninsular War*. For Scott the *Register* became a vehicle for such things as his enthusiasm for military strategy, in "Cursory Remarks upon the French Order of Battle," and a bit of critical silliness in his "Of the Living Poets of Great Britain," identifying Thomas Campbell, Southey, and Scott himself ("the minion of modern popularity") as the greatest of living poets, compared to whom Byron is ignored, Coleridge is almost unmentionable ("such a mixture of the terrible with the disgusting"), and Wordsworth is "an unsuccessful competitor for poetic fame."[79]

From the start, however, the firm of John Ballantyne did not do well financially, a condition seriously aggravated, as Constable had foreseen, by the ambitious undertaking just described, and in 1813 Scott negotiated a bailout with Constable, who agreed to take over Ballantyne's stock, including the *Annual Register,* in return for a share in Scott's work and a pledge that the Ballantyne firm would be wound up as soon as possible. As part of the deal, it was agreed that Ballantyne was to have a share in the profits of the Waverley Novels. In addition, in 1820, Scott offered his services as editor of a *Novelist's Library*, to be published, for Ballantyne's benefit, by the short-lived firm of Hurst, Robinson in London and printed by brother James Ballantyne's press in Edinburgh. Set up in 1818 by a former partner in Longman's and the brother of a bookseller in Leeds, Hurst, Robinson collapsed in the financial crash of 1826, to which Constable also succumbed temporarily. In its brief existence, however, the firm did publish the *Novelist's Library* (1821-24) consisting of ten substantial volumes of about 800 pages each, with brief biographical information and twenty to thirty pages of critical notices by Scott on each of the authors represented.

The first volume opened with an "Advertisement" (in the sense of the French "Avertissement") outlining the aim and scope of the project.

> It is intended to reprint, in the present form, the Works of the best English Novelists, together with selections from the German, French, and Italian (some of which are already translated and others in the course of translation), with Memoirs of the Authors' Lives, and Criticism on their Writings prefixed. The Works of each Author will be published separately and complete, in a single volume, as in the present instance, or in two or more, as the length of the composition shall require.

Volume 1 (1821), "The Novels of Henry Fielding, Esq.," contained the texts of *Joseph Andrews, Tom Jones, Amelia,* and *Jonathan Wild.* Volume 2 (1821) was devoted to Tobias Smollett (*Roderick Random, Peregrine Pickle, Humphrey Clinker*); Volume 3 (1821) also to Smollett (*Count Fathom, Sir Launcelot Greaves*) and a translation of Cervantes's *Don Quixote*; Volume 4 (1822) to Le Sage (*Gil Blas* and *The Devil on Two Sticks* [*Le Diable boiteux*] in Smollett's translations) and Charles Johnstone (*The Adventures of a Guinea*); Volume 5 (1823) to Sterne (*Tristram Shandy, A Sentimental Journey*), Oliver Goldsmith (*The Vicar of Wakefield*), Dr. Johnson (*Rasselas*), Henry Mackenzie (*The Man of Feeling, The Man of the World, Julia de Roubigné*), Horace Walpole (*The Castle of Otranto*), and the eighteenth-century novelist Clara Reeve (*The Old English Baron*); Volumes 6, 7, and 8 (1824) to "the novels of Samuel Richardson, Esq." (*Pamela, Clarissa, Sir Charles Grandison*); Vol. 9 to Swift (*Gulliver's Travels*), Robert Bage (*Mount Henneth, Barham Downs, James Wallace*), and Richard Cumberland (*Henry*); and Vol. 10 (1824) to Mrs. Ann Radcliffe (*The Sicilian Romance, The Romance of the Forest, The Mysteries of Udolpho, The Italian,* and *Castles of Athlin and Dunbayne*).

The title page of the first two volumes carried the notice "London: Published by Hurst, Robinson, and Co. Printed by James Ballantyne and Company, At the Border Press. For John Ballantyne, Edinburgh." The volumes published after John Ballantyne's death in 1821 omit the reference to him and add "Edinburgh" to "At the Border Press." The publishing house of John Ballantyne, such as it was, had clearly ceased to exist.

William Blackwood (Edinburgh) 1810

The son of a silk merchant, William Blackwood, the founder of the firm that bears his name, was born in Edinburgh in 1776, received a sound education, and at the age of fourteen began a six-year apprenticeship with Bell & Bradfute, the Edinburgh bookseller and publisher (q.v.). He gained experience in other areas of the book trade as superintendent of the Glasgow branch of another Edinburgh publisher and by working with antiquarian booksellers and auctioneers in Edinburgh and London. In 1804 he opened a shop of his own in Edinburgh, specializing in rare and antiquarian books. By 1810 he had begun branching out into publishing, producing historical and religious works for the Scottish market and books on travel and exploration. In 1811 he also became the Edinburgh agent for London-based publishers, such as John Murray (q.v.) and Thomas Cadell, and in 1813 he established a link to the Ballantynes, Walter Scott's printers. These connections paved the way for Blackwood to figure as co-publisher with Murray of Cantos I and II of Byron's *Childe Harold's Pilgrimage* in 1812 and Scott's *Tales of My Landlord* (*Old Mortality* and *The Black Dwarf*) in 1816, and as co-publisher with Cadell of Shelley's *Prometheus Unbound* in 1820, and Hazlitt's *Table-Talk* in 1821—despite the attacks on both Shelley and Hazlitt in Blackwood's popular and widely read *Magazine*.

William Blackwood launched his *Magazine* in 1817. It was intended in part as a Tory-inclined rival to Archibald Constable's Whig-inclined *Edinburgh Review* and as competition to the ailing (but in fact, to a modern reader, remarkably wide-ranging) *Scots Magazine and Edinburgh Literary Miscellany* (as of August 1817, *The Edinburgh Magazine and Literary Miscellany*), which was also put out by Constable. Blackwood's *Edinburgh Monthly Magazine* did not do particularly well at first, with sales of only twenty-five hundred copies per issue, but re-launched six months later under new editorship and with a slightly altered title, *Blackwood's Edinburgh Magazine*—commonly referred to simply as *Blackwood's*—quickly became the flagship publication of the Blackwood firm. By 1827, sales had climbed to sixty-three hundred copies and the magazine was soon attracting many major writers, whose works the firm subsequently put out in independent volumes. *Blackwood's* remained consistently conservative politically. The July issue of 1850, for example, contained articles opposing free trade, along with a fierce attack—reminiscent of the hostile pamphlets provoked a century earlier by the so-called "Jew Bill" (Jewish Naturalisation Act) of 1753, which would have permitted persons professing the Jewish religion born outside England to be naturalized by Parliament, without having to receive the Sacrament of the Lord's Supper, and which had to be repealed the following year because of the storm of protest it unleashed—on a bill passed by the Commons in 1848 but voted down by the Lords in 1850 that would have allowed Lionel de Rothschild to take his seat in Parliament without having to take a Christian oath. Ten years later, in Volume LXXX (January 1860), an essay titled "Rambles at Random in the Southern States" aimed to contradict the widespread opinion in Britain that "misery is the rule and happiness the exception with the negro in the Southern States of America" (p. 106). Nevertheless, articles ranged widely. In the very first issue (April 1817), for instance, there were essays on "Banks for Saving," "The Sculpture of the Greeks," "Greek Tragedy," "The Present State of the City of Venice," "The Culture of the Sugar Cane in the United States," and "Scottish Gypsies." In its newer incarnation as *Blackwood's Edinburgh Magazine*, Keats, Shelley, Tennyson, Wordsworth, and Coleridge were reviewed or discussed frequently, the last-named in particular being the object of severe criticisms, to which the poet responded. At one point the viciousness of Lockhart's and the Irishman William Maginn's many attacks on what they called the "Cockney School of Poetry"—that is, a group of liberal writers, mostly from London, that included Hazlitt, Leigh Hunt, and "the less important members," namely, "the Shelleys, the Keatses"— threatened to end in a lawsuit. (In Murray's similarly conservative *Quarterly Review* for April 1818 a comparably scathing and disrespectful attack by the Irish statesman and literary critic John

Wilson Croker on Keats's *Endymion* was blamed by Shelley for hastening the poet's death in 1821.) Thereafter the tone was moderated and by 1832 Coleridge could write Blackwell that "*Blackwood's Magazine* [...] is an unprecedented Phenomenon in the world of letters and forms the golden—alas! the only—remaining link between the Periodical Press and the enduring literature of Great Britain."[80] Under the more benign editorship of Alexander and then John Blackwood, the founder's sons, Elizabeth Barrett Browning was one of the poets whose work now appeared in *Blackwood's*, most notably *The Cry of the Children* in the August 1843 issue (vol. 54).

De Quincey's *On Murder Considered as One of the Fine Arts* appeared in the magazine in 1827 with follow-ups in 1839 and 1854; his *The English Mail-Coach* in October and December 1849. But it was on John Blackwood's becoming director of the firm a few years after the death, in 1834, of his father that Blackwood really took off as a publisher of fine literature. John Blackwood, known from boyhood as "the little Editor,"[81] emerges from the study of the firm's history by his longtime assistant, the prolific novelist Margaret Oliphant, and his daughter Mary Porter, and, above all, from the correspondence reproduced in their volumes, as a man deeply and knowledgeably engaged with the literature of his time, a good friend of many writers, including some, like Thackeray, who did not publish with him—the great novelist was the guest of the Blackwoods at their Edinburgh home on Randolph Crescent in 1857 when he came north to give his talks on "the Georges" to the Edinburgh Philosophical Institution—and a thoughtful supporter and, at times, constructive critic of those who did.

Among works of fiction that were first published in installments in *Blackwood's*, after John took over as editor, the novels of George Eliot, whom John Blackwood admired greatly and with whom he developed a relation of close friendship, figure prominently.[82] *Scenes of Clerical Life* appeared in 1857–58, *Adam Bede* in 1859. The following year, Eliot, who by now had achieved considerable popular success, refused to allow *The Mill on the Floss* (title suggested by Blackwood) to be serialized in the magazine since its publication there, she said, "would sweep away

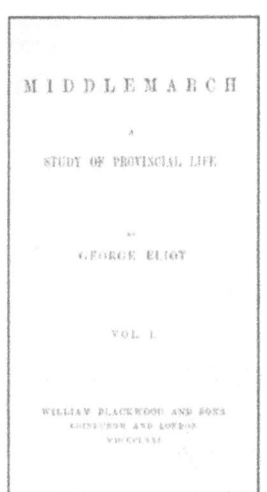

perhaps 20,000—nay, 40,000—readers who would otherwise demand copies of the complete work." That, together with Eliot's switch to Smith, Elder for *Romola,* led to a brief cooling off of the author–publisher relation. Nevertheless, touched by the courteous and understanding letter to her in which John Blackwood expressed his disappointment over *Romola,* Eliot returned to Blackwood with *Silas Marner* (1861), *Felix Holt the Radical* (1866), *Middlemarch* (1871–72), and *Daniel Deronda* (1876)—all first published in installments in the magazine and then, many times over the years, in different book formats ranging from inexpensive to de luxe, as well as in the multiple editions of Eliot's complete *Works* that were put out by Blackwood.

The individual volumes of Eliot's novels and the multivolume editions of her *Works,* though printed in large numbers, sold very well, delivering handsome profits to the firm.[83] Even the long, 300-page narrative poem to which she gave the title *The Spanish Gypsy* and that Blackwood put out in 1868, having "shown great delight" when she first read him part of it over dinner in June 1867, went through three printings before the year was out. On learning, in late October 1879, that John Blackwood was "dangerously ill" and that "there is little hope of recovery" (he died the following day), Eliot wrote to Charles Lewes, the son of her life's partner, George Henry Lewes, that "he will be a heavy loss to me" as "he has been bound up with what I most cared for in my life for more than twenty years and his good qualities have made many things easy for me that without him would often have been difficult."[84]

Blackwood also entertained excellent relations with Anthony Trollope, who, along with his wife, was the Blackwoods' guest at their summer home near St. Andrews in 1868 and subsequently went on a trip with them to the Isle of Skye.[85] Trollope's *Nina*

Balatka and *Linda Tressel* were serialized in the magazine in 1867 and 1868, and, also in 1868, Blackwood persuaded the novelist to abridge Julius Caesar's *Commentaries on the Gallic War* (*De Bello Gallico*) for his new series of inexpensive "Ancient Classics for English Readers." Of this project, Trollope wrote Blackwood that "it was a tough bit of work but I have enjoyed it amazingly."[86] In a charming letter, dated May 7, 1868, he made a present of the copyright to his publisher and friend on the occasion of Blackwood's upcoming June 1 birthday. Trollope's dystopian *The Fixed Period* appeared in the pages of the magazine somewhat later (1881–82), shortly after John Blackwood's death.

With Bulwer-Lytton, John Blackwood enjoyed no less friendly relations and, although most of the statesman-writer's popular publications were already behind him, Blackwood published one of his last works, the odd science fiction fantasy entitled *The Coming Race*, despite his misgivings about Bulwer-Lytton's insistence that it appear anonymously. The earliest version was indeed published anonymously in May 1871 and turned out to be quite a success. "Blackwood tells me that the opinions he hears privately are very enthusiastic," Bulwer-Lytton wrote, "chiefly from professors and scholars, and the papers usually most hostile to me are wonderfully civil to it, Spectator, Examiner, Athenaeum, Scotsman all my wonted foes." On January 30, 1872, he informed his son that "*The Coming Race* has had a great sale five editions, 1871, and is now going into a cheaper one."[87] Later editions, put out in 1872 and 1873, did finally carry the name of the author, who died in 1873. *The Parisians*, a political satire, was serialized in the magazine between October 1872 and January 1874, and published in a separate edition in four volumes in 1873. Finally, *Kenelm Chillingly, His Adventures and Opinions*, Bulwer-Lytton's last novel, was published posthumously by Blackwood in 1873.

Joseph Conrad was another Blackwood author, though not a notably faithful one. Following two early novels (*Almayer's Folly*, published by T. Fisher Unwin in 1895 and *An Outcast of the Islands*, put out by the same publisher in 1896), and a few short stories —"The Idiots" in Arthur Symons' *Savoy* (October 1896), "The Lagoon" in *The Cornhill* (January 1897), "A Victim of Progress," later retitled "An Outpost of Progress," in *Cosmopolis* (June–July 1897), and a serialized version of *The Nigger of the 'Narcissus,'* which had been rejected by Unwin, in Heinemann's *New Review* (August through December, 1897)—he succeeded in getting the short tale *Karain: A Memory* accepted for publication in *Blackwood's* in 1897. It had not been easy. William Blackwood III, who succeeded his uncle John as editor of the journal, could be "extremely dilatory in answering or in coming to a decision about a manuscript" (as George Bernard Shaw was to discover somewhat later),[88] and had kept Conrad on the hook for at least two months, before following the strong recommendation of a trusted adviser, David Storrar Meldrum, and accepting Conrad's manuscript.[89] Besides, Blackwood offered considerably less in payment than Conrad had asked (£16 instead of £40). Still, as Conrad was hard up for money and still had to struggle at this point in his career to get his work into print, he was thrilled to be featured in a prestigious and widely read magazine and elated by Blackwood's request that he be given "the first refusal of any short story I may write." "This, coming from Modern Athens [i.e., Edinburgh], was so flattering that for a whole day I walked about with my nose in the air," he wrote his friend E. L. Sanderson, on July 19, 1897.[90] As he had already committed *The Nigger of the "Narcissus"* to Heinemann's *New Review* and had also promised *The Rescue*, the novel he was working on, to Heinemann (in fact he had a hard time with this work and finished it only toward the end of his life, in 1920), he expressed regret in a letter to Blackwood that "it will not be my good fortune to appear serially in the pages of Maga" (the popular nickname for *Blackwood's Magazine*). At the same time he was careful to keep the door open for other future submissions: "Till you expressly decline, I consider myself authorized to send you any short story or sketch I may write."[91] The short story "Youth" followed in the September 1898 issue of *Blackwood's*, whereas the first installment of the novel *The Heart of Darkness* was given the honor of appearing in the double, one thousandth number of

the magazine issued in February 1899, with subsequent installments continuing through the April issue. *Lord Jim* was published serially between October 1899 and November 1900, followed by *The End of the Tether* in the issues from July to December 1902. Blackwood also published all of Conrad's works as separate volumes soon after their appearance in the magazine. On the whole, Conrad was pleased. On December 30, 1900, he sent William Blackwood his "best wishes for the New Year and for the New Century. You have made the last year of the Old Century very memorable for me by your kindness. I am alluding to the production of 'Lord Jim.' [. . .] I can't think of that work without thinking of you. As it went on, I appreciated more and more your helpful words, your helpful silences and your helpful acts; and this feeling shall never grow old, or cold, or faint."[92]

By 1902–03, however, Conrad was in a sea of troubles. He was ill, his wife was also ill and he had to tend to her; he needed Blackwood to advance him money or act as security for loans to enable him to struggle along; and he continued to write for other publications, which made him late with copy promised for "Maga." At that point the relationship with Blackwood began to unravel. In December 1902, Conrad reassured Blackwood that he would soon "have something to knock at Maga's door with." But perhaps by then "you won't have me?" he added, following up that reflection with a gentle warning, veiled in irony: "But let me tell you that I am no longer obscure. A publication called the 'Smart Set'—heavens! What a name—has asked me, this very day, for a short story of 3–4 thou. words."[93] Around 1902 Conrad began entrusting negotiations with various publishers, including Blackwood, to the literary agent James B. Pinker and this drove a new wedge into the Blackwood–Conrad connection. By 1905 the fairly close and personal relationship of publisher and writer and the correspondence they had engaged in had essentially come to an end, with Pinker having taken Conrad's place in corresponding with Blackwood.[94] As the author of a history of the publishing house of Blackwood put it,

> William had exercised much patience with Conrad, taking infinite pains to nurse him along, lending him money against stories not

yet written, and experiencing trouble with the make-up of "Maga" when promised stories did not arrive. Conrad agreed to repay a loan by writing three stories, but only two that satisfied William were supplied. By 1903 Conrad's letters had become very brief; and then they ceased.[95]

Later work of Conrad's appeared in *The Pall Mall Magazine, The English Review, The London Review, The Fortnightly Magazine,* and many other publications in Britain, the United States, and other countries. The old connection with "Maga" was not renewed. Conrad himself noted that "*Blackwood's,* since the old man [i.e., William Blackwood] retired, do not much care for my work."[96] At one point he observed appreciatively in a letter to J. S. Meldrum, who had been his strong supporter at Blackwood's, that, though "to appear in P.[all] M. [all] M[agazine] and the Ill. Lond. News"—successes he attributed to the interventions of his agent Pinker—"is advantageous [...] I only care for Maga, my first and only Love!"[97] In fact, however, none of the many novels and stories Conrad produced after *The End of the Tether* was published by Blackwood.

As a Scottish publisher, Blackwood inevitably did his part in putting out works by Scots writers, notably John Galt and James Hogg,[98] and, in a tradition well established among Scottish publishers, foreign writers in translation, such as Friedrich Schlegel's *Lectures on the History of Literature* (1818, 1841), Goethe's *Poems and Ballads* (1859) and *Faust* (1866), and Heine's *Poems and Ballads* (1878).

In general, however, Blackwood seems not to have played the significant role in nurturing the literature of the twentieth century that the company had played in nurturing that of the nineteenth, when its policy does indeed appear to have been one of "fostering literary genius," in the words of the author of a recent company history.[99] William Blackwood's successor, George Blackwood, it has been said, had neither the keen literary interests of his predecessor, nor the latter's desire to establish and maintain personal relations with his authors. Although the firm successfully recruited a John Buchan (*The Thirty-Nine Steps,* 1915), it missed out on George Bernard Shaw, whose first submission, *Immaturity*, was turned down. Thomas Hardy, Robert Louis Stevenson, and H. G. Wells also failed to place their work with the firm. Blackwood did publish E. M. Forster's first novel, *Where Angels Fear to Tread*, in August 1905. Its modest sales, however, led to a royalties offer for Forster's next book, *The Longest Journey* (1907), that left the novelist feeling shortchanged. "Am quarrelling with Blackwood," he wrote, "and I think I shall have to go elsewhere." Though the disagreement was patched over, sales of *The Longest Journey* were not encouraging either and were not advanced by a low-key promotional campaign. Viewing Forster as one of their less successful popular novelists, the firm spent very little on advertising and promoting his work.[100] For his next novel, *A Room with a View*, Forster therefore turned to another publisher, Edward Arnold, with whom *Howard's End* and *A Passage to India* then also appeared.

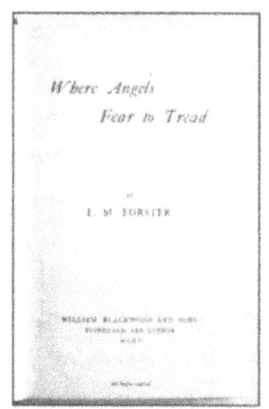

Smith & Elder (London) 1816

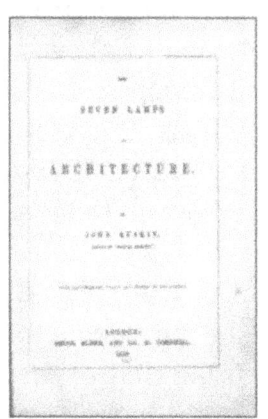

Born in 1789 to a small landowner in Morayshire, in the Northeast of Scotland, George Smith served an apprenticeship with a bookseller in Elgin, the county capital, before taking the high road south to London, where he found employment in the publishing house of Rivington, moving soon after to a better job in the house of fellow-Scot John Murray (q.v.), with whom he remained on friendly terms until the latter's death in 1843. In 1816, Smith joined with Alexander Elder, another immigrant to London from Scotland's Northeast (Elder was a native of Banff in Aberdeenshire) in setting up a partnership as Smith & Elder, booksellers and stationers, with a small shop in Fenchurch Street. For the first three years the business kept to this original design, selling paper, pens, pencils, ink, account books, and similar stationery items, as well as books, new and used (Fénelon's *Works*, Mackenzie's *Works*, Burns, Scott, *The Beauties of Sterne*), journals (the *Quarterly Review*, the *Edinburgh Review*), and musical scores, especially Scottish airs. An intense and profitable trade was developed with officers in the service of the East India Company and this growing connection contributed significantly to the firm's financial strength and success over the years. In the words of Smith's son, George Murray Smith, who took over the leadership of the firm and brought it to prominence, "sixty years ago, the business of Smith, Elder & Co. consisted chiefly of an export trade to India and our colonies. There was also a small publishing business, occasionally involving a certain amount of enterprise" or, as a more recent historian of the company explained, "For half of its existence," publishing "was but one department of a vast business, one enterprise among the many which were directed by the same head." Smith, Elder & Co. were "East India agents, bankers, and publishers."[101] There was certainly no reason in 1816 to anticipate that a relatively poor lad from Morayshire and his slightly less impecunious friend from Banff, albeit the latter did have strong literary leanings, would turn out to have founded a business that did as much as Smith, Elder was to do to promote English literature in the nineteenth century.

Three years after setting up their stationery business the partners added publishing to their other activities—still in a modest way—when they put out *Sermons and Expositions on Interesting Portions of Scripture* by John Morison, a Congregational minister (1819). Five years after that, in 1824, the firm having acquired a third partner, one Patrick Stewart, and renamed itself Smith, Elder & Co., and a son, George Murray Smith, having been born to George Smith, the Smith family and the business moved to more commodious quarters at 65 Cornhill. As gift books were popular as "keepsakes" with well-to-do readers in the 1820s and 1830s, the new company made the decision in 1824 to take over production of *Friendship's Offering*, a fashionable and elaborately illustrated annual gift book, first published in 1824 by a neighboring publisher, Lupton Relfe, of 13 Cornhill. This venture proved extremely successful. Featuring poetry and prose by Coleridge, the so-called "peasant poet" John Clare, John Galt, James

Hogg ("The Ettrick Shepherd"), John Ruskin (his first publication), Robert Southey, and the women poets Mary Howitt and Mary Russell Mitford, it sold between eight and ten thousand copies annually over the years from 1824 to 1844, despite its relatively high price of twelve shillings. A couple of expensive books of illustrations—*Views of Calcutta, engraved by Robert Havell* (1824–26) made up of sixteen engravings of colored aquatints by Scottish artist James Baillie Fraser, and Richard Thomson's *Chronicles of London Bridge* (1827), consisting of 56 wood engravings—were also put out, the former at the extremely high price of 16 guineas and the latter at a still fairly steep 28 shillings. In 1826 *A New Greek and English Lexikon* was published jointly with Chalmers and Collins of Glasgow and won favor as a useful and reliable work of reference. In contrast, a "Library of Romance," launched in 1833 and intended to be a series of novels, each one presented in a single volume, at a modest price, as distinct from the customary practice of three-volume novels, was a failure and had to be discontinued. Only fifteen volumes were published, most by little-known authors, with the exception of Victor Hugo (*The Slave King*, a translation of his *Bug Jargal*), and John Galt (*The Stolen Child*).[102]

The first major original publication of Smith, Elder & Co. came a decade later, thanks to Smith's son, George Murray Smith (Murray was the name of his mother's family), who had joined the firm in 1838, at the age of fourteen, and worked his way up in it until, at nineteen, he was made head of the still very modest publishing department and given £1500 to use at his discretion. A 30-year relationship—more than that, a close friendship—with John Ruskin began when George Murray Smith agreed to publish the first volume of *Modern Painters* in 1843, after Ruskin's father undertook to compensate the firm for any financial loss. This was followed by the second volume in 1846 and the third and fourth volumes in 1853 and 1856; by *The Seven Lamps of Architecture* in 1849; the three volumes of *The Stones of Venice* in 1851 and 1853; the provocative essay volume *Unto this Last* in 1862 (originally a series of articles published in 1860 in Smith and Elder's *Cornhill* Magazine); and *Fors Clavigera* in 1871. Between 1843 and 1872, Smith, Elder & Co. put out forty volumes by Ruskin.[103]

The year 1844 saw the publication of Leigh Hunt's *Imagination and Fancy; or, Selections from the English Poets with an Essay in Answer to the Question What is Poetry*. After turning down, as several other publishers had already done, Charlotte Brontë's *The Professor*, George Murray Smith—by now, after the death of his father and the retirement of Alexander Elder, the head of the firm—accepted *Jane Eyre*, which Brontë submitted to the company because of the "courteous" and "considerate" rejection letter she had received for *The Professor*, and which Smith spent one entire Sunday reading without being able to "put the book down."[104] He succeeded in bringing the novel out, under the pseudonym, on which Brontë insisted, of Currer Bell, in only six weeks, in time for the 1847 Christmas trade. *Jane Eyre* was followed by *Shirley* in 1849 and *Villette* in 1853. In 1857, two years after Charlotte Brontë's death, Smith, Elder published *The Professor*. In addition, *Poems by Currer, Ellis, and Acton Bell* (pseudonyms of the three Brontë sisters), originally published privately in 1846, was republished by Smith, Elder in 1850. Almost from the start the relationship between publisher and author, George

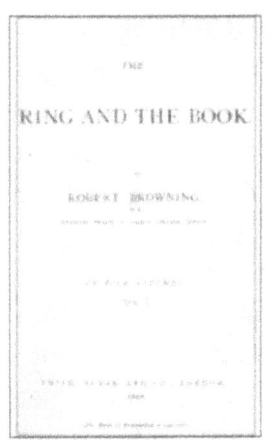

Murrray Smith and Charlotte Brontë, was an intensely personal one, with affection and admiration on both sides, and much time spent in each other's company.[105] In June 1850, when Brontë was visiting Smith and his mother, who were then living in Gloucester Terrace in the West End of London, Smith persuaded the writer to sit for a portrait by the fashionable artist George Richmond and sent the finished painting as a gift to her father.[106]

After Brontë's death, for a fee of £600 (raised subsequently to £800), Smith commissioned Mrs. Gaskell, the admired author of the highly successful novel *Mary Barton* (1848), to write a *Life of Charlotte Brontë*, which came out in 1857. Mrs. Gaskell then switched from her previous publisher, Chapman and Hall—which had paid her £100 for the copyright of *Mary Barton* and, following the popular and critical success of that first novel, had also put out *North and South* (1854–55) and *Round the Sofa* (1859)—to Smith, Elder. *Sylvia's Lovers* was published in 1863, *A Dark Night's Work* also in 1863, *Cousin Phillis* in 1864, and *Wives and Daughters* in 1865. Both the Brontë novels and those of Elizabeth Gaskell went through many editions.

George Murray Smith also managed to draw Robert Browning, William Makepeace Thackeray, and, for a brief period, Anthony Trollope from Chapman and Hall to the house of Smith, Elder. The first two benefited considerably from the change.[107] Smith's publication of Browning's *The Ring and the Book* in 1868, it has been said, with a second edition in 1869, transformed a hitherto neglected poet who had not been well treated by his previous publisher, into "a star of the first magnitude."[108] A decade before that, in 1859, Smith decided to start a monthly literary magazine, to be called *The Cornhill* (after the firm's address), and persuaded Thackeray to provide a serialized novel for it. After his first attempts to find an editor for the new venture were unsuccessful, Smith asked Thackeray, whose *The Kickleburys on the Rhine*, *Henry Esmond*, *English Humourists of the Eighteenth Century*, and *The Rose and the Ring* he had published in 1850, 1852, 1853 and 1855, respectively, if he would take on the job himself and Thackeray agreed to do so, provided his responsibility was limited to the editorial side of the magazine and did not extend to the business side. Smith was convinced, correctly as it turned out, that "a shilling magazine, which contained, in addition to other first-class literary matter, a serial novel by Thackeray must command a large sale." In addition, he had resolved to recruit "the most brilliant contributors from every quarter" and, buoyed by his lucrative India trade, to offer them lavish payments. As he himself recalled, "No pains and no cost were spared to make the new magazine the best periodical yet known to English literature. Our terms were lavish to the point of recklessness."[109] Thackeray's salary as editor, for instance, was to be £1,000 a year, whereas for the rights to his own contributions of one or two novels in twelve monthly installments and their subsequent publication as separate volumes, he was to receive £350 each month.[110] For the first year's issues of the magazine, Thackeray, as editor, commissioned Anthony Trollope to write the second serial, to accompany his own. The first volume of *The Cornhill* (six handsomely illustrated issues from January to June 1860) thus contained both Trollope's *Framley Parsonage*, for which he was paid £1,000—twice as much as he had ever received previously—and Thackeray's own *Lovel the Widower* (published by Smith, Elder & Co. in book form the following year), as well as essays by Thackeray and, among others, George Henry Lewes, the companion of George Eliot.[111] Many stories and essays were unsigned and that policy continued into the 1890s. As the historian of the company observes, and as has been noted earlier in the present essay, anonymity was quite usual, except for eminent poets or deceased authors, such as the Brontës. Even Trollope's serial in the early issues of the *Cornhill* was anonymous, his name appearing only in the last installment (1864).[112]

Thackeray also wrote *The Adventures of Philip* and *The Roundabout Papers* for early issues of the new magazine. Though Chapman and Hall did not lose him completely, it was being published in the *Cornhill* that raised Thackeray's literary reputation and his earning power[113] and he remained in his editorial position for another two years, until 1862. The first issue of the magazine was a phenomenal success. It sold 120,000 copies, "a number then without precedent in English serial literature," according to Smith himself,[114] and the first year saw the appearance, in addition to the novels of Trollope and Thackeray, of Ruskin's *Unto this Last*, the opening chapters of Charlotte Brontë's unfinished novel *Emma*, with an introduction by Thackeray, and poems by Matthew Arnold ("Men of Genius"), Charlotte Brontë ("Watching and Wishing"), Emily Brontë ("The Outcast Mother," published posthumously), Elizabeth Barrett Browning ("A Musical Instrument" and "A Forced Recruit at Solferino"), Washington Irving ("Written in the Deepdene Album"), and Tennyson ("Tithonus"). Like Murray and Strahan before him, Smith was deeply involved personally with his authors. As already noted, Charlotte Brontë became a close friend and was a frequent visitor to the home of Smith and his mother; Smith was often a guest of the

Ruskins, both father and son, and they were likewise guests of his. Browning and Smith were on intimate terms and on his deathbed Browning bade his son seek George Smith's advice whenever he had need of wise counsel. Smith superintended the arrangements for Browning's funeral in Westminster Abbey on December 1, 1889, and served as one of the deceased poet's pallbearers.

In the first year of the twentieth century, shortly before his own death, Smith recalled with obvious pleasure, in his "Reminiscences," how "we lightened our labours in the service of the Cornhill by monthly dinners. The principal contributors used to assemble at my table in Gloucester Square every month . . . and these 'Cornhill dinners' were very delightful and interesting. Thackeray always attended, though he was often in an indifferent state of health."[115] In 1863, the hospitality Smith offered his authors and collaborators took a new form. Having acquired Oak Hill Lodge, a house in Hampstead where he spent the summers, he and Mrs. Smith issued a general invitation to their literary friends to dine at Hampstead on any Friday they chose without giving notice. The number of guests varied, reaching as many as forty. Among the most regular were Thackeray, Trollope, Wilkie Collins, the painter John Everett Millais, and the illustrator and caricaturist John Leech. On one occasion the guests included Russian novelist Ivan Turgenev. Smith's warm relationship with his authors is well summarized in a recent study of the *Cornhill Magazine*:

> His clients were attracted to his practical attitude, his sound counsel, his consistent generosity, courtesy, and honesty in his dealings with them. It is almost impossible to find an instance when a Smith, Elder writer looked back with anything but affection and respect for his publisher. In the highly competitive London publishing market, Smith was able to secure long-standing loyalties from Charlotte Brontë, Thackeray, Mrs. Gaskell, Trollope, Wilkie Collins, Ruskin, Charles Darwin, the Brownings, Arnold, John Addington Symonds, and others of equal prominence. Beginning his direction of publishing affairs at age nineteen, he became Charlotte Brontë's publisher at age twenty-four, one of Thackeray's publishers by the time he was twenty-six, and Mrs. Gaskell's family friend and adviser before he was thirty.[116]

Within a few years, however, circulation of the *Cornhill* began to drop. May 1862 saw the initial print run reduced by half to 60,000 copies, and Thackeray resigned as editor, in part because he was unhappy with Smith's intrusions into editorial matters (his acceptance, for instance, of novels Thackeray would not have accepted and his habit of often enclosing money in the rejection letters sent to indigent women writers) and disapproved in particular of Smith's extravagant offer of £10,000 to George Eliot for *Romola*. (In fact, she received £7,000, but that was still an exceptional sum.) After vainly attempting to replace Thackeray with Robert Browning and Lewes, an editorial committee of three was formed, of which Lewes and Smith himself were stable members. Even though the magazine was now (since 1863) losing money, Smith continued to support it with funds from his other successful businesses (among them Appolinaris, the popular "Queen of Table Waters"!) and it did continue not only to publish old contributors, such as Ruskin, Trollope (*The Small House at Allington*, 1862–64), Matthew Arnold (*Anarchy and Authority*, 1868, retitled *Culture and Anarchy* as a stand-alone book), and Thackeray himself (posthumously, in 1864, the uncompleted *Denis Duval*), but to recruit new novelists and essayists, such as Mrs. Gaskell (*Cousin Phillis*, 1864, *Wives and Daughters*, 1864–66), Wilkie Collins (*Armadale*, 1864–66) and Charles Reade (*Put Yourself in His Place*, 1870), while at the same time attracting others to the firm's book-publishing business, not least Queen Victoria, whose *Leaves from the Journal of our Life in the Highlands* was published by Smith, Elder in December 1867 and again, the following year, in an inexpensive popular edition costing only two shillings and sixpence. *More Leaves from the Journal of our Life in the Highlands from 1862 to 1882* followed in 1884.

In 1871, Smith persuaded Leslie Stephen, not yet the father of Virginia Woolf, to take on the editorship of *The Cornhill*. Under Stephen's direction, the magazine published Thomas Hardy's *Far from the Madding Crowd* (1871–74), George Meredith's *The Adven-*

tures of Harry Richmond (1871), Henry James's *Daisy Miller* (June and July 1879) and *Washington Square* (June to November, 1881). To these were added, at a later stage and under different direction, Arthur Conan Doyle's *The White Company* (1891) and Joseph Conrad's short story "Lagoon" (1897).

Meantime, beginning in the mid-1860s, Smith, Elder opened up another new path in literary publishing with a series of standard novels, by contemporary authors such as Thackeray, the Brontës, Wilkie Collins, and George Meredith, in a variety of formats at various, but relatively modest prices: an "Illustrated Library" series of twenty-two volumes (1867–70), a "Popular" series of twelve volumes (1872–73), a "De Luxe" series of twenty-four volumes (1879), and a "Pocket" series of twenty-seven volumes (1886–87).

The company founded by two lads from the Northeast of Scotland was thus a major influence in both the promotion and the dissemination of nineteenth-century English literature. Finally, in the last two decades of his life, George Murray Smith came up with the idea of a dictionary of national history, which, after consultation with Leslie Stephen, who agreed to serve as editor, was reconceived as a *Dictionary of National Biography*—one of at least three fundamental, enduring, and constantly re-edited English-language reference works (the other two being the *Encyclopaedia Britannica* and Grove's *Dictionary of Music*) invented and produced by Scottish publishers. The sixty volumes of the first edition of the *DNB* came out between 1885 and 1900. Smith died in 1901.

William Collins (Glasgow) 1819

Even more passionately committed to religion and morality, if that is possible, than the founder of the Nelson company in Edinburgh, William Collins, founder of the huge Glasgow firm of publishers bearing his name, was born in 1789 in Pollokshaws, now a district in Glasgow's South Side, but still at that time a village, with a cluster of cloth mills and dye works, in the agricultural Renfrewshire parish of Eastwood. His parents could apparently afford to send him to the local parish school for a few years, where Collins became the star pupil, noted for his "diligence and ability," by the schoolmaster, whom he in turn loved and revered. The parish minister, a frequent visitor to the school, also won the pupil's affection and trust, encouraged him in boyhood and adolescence, and gave him assistance and advice in the critical years of his young manhood. Shortly after reaching the age of eleven or twelve, Collins went to work at the loom in Pollokshaws—at the time there were fourteen thousand looms within thirty miles of Glasgow Cross—and was soon offering his workmates religious instruction on Sundays and lessons in English, writing, and arithmetic on weeknights after the mills had closed. This activity drew the attention of his former parish minister, now minister of St. George's Tron Church, situated in the heart of Glasgow and frequented by the wealthy local merchants, with the result that in 1813 Collins was in a position to give up work in the mill to concentrate on a career in education, and to open a private school, with a nucleus of twenty boarders, in the city center. English, writing, and arithmetic were taught at the school's three divisions: a day school and two evening schools. Collins so impressed the local Tron church leadership that at the unusually young age of twenty-five he was made an elder of the church. By this time, he had also acquired a wife, the daughter of a well-to-do engineer in nearby Paisley.[117] His commitment to his Christian faith never wavered and led him to embrace and ardently promote, among other moral causes, the temperance movement in Britain. He was a founder of Britain's first Temperance Society and gave speeches on the topic all over Scotland and, as the movement spread, England too.[118]

The turning point in Collins's career resulted from a visit in the first year of his eldership to the Fife village of Kilmany, where Thomas Chalmers, the passionate and gifted evangelist, Collins's senior by ten years but then still at the start of his amazing life's trajectory, was the local minister. An article by Chalmers on the evidences of Christianity in the *Edinburgh Encyclopaedia* had made such a deep impression on Collins that he undertook the long journey by coach in order to hear Chalmers preach. He was so moved by what he heard that he could not rest until he had prevailed on his fellow elders—overcoming the resistance of the

Lord Provost and others by organizing a petition signed by two hundred leading members of the congregation—to have Chalmers translated to the Tron Church, the minister of which had just been appointed to a chair at Glasgow University. Chalmers arrived in Glasgow in 1815 and his preaching drew crowds to the Tron Church; it was not unusual for a throng of two thousand to press into a building designed to accommodate fourteen hundred. Meanwhile, on his side, Collins—whose revenue from his schools had reached a considerable sum—had opened, in his own house, the first of a chain of Sunday schools that secured the attendance of twelve hundred children within a couple of years. The publishing house of Collins arose from the close personal friendship that developed between teacher and preacher, Collins and Chalmers, and from their shared faith and values.

Chalmers's success as an evangelical theologian and preacher at the Tron Church soon led to his weekday sermons being collected into a single volume entitled *Astronomical Discourses* and published in 1817 by the long-established Glasgow bookseller John Smith. (Founded in 1751, with premises in the Trongate, then at the center of the old city of Glasgow, the Smith bookstore is one of the oldest, possibly the oldest continuously operating bookstore in the English-speaking world, having moved in 1907 to handsome and spacious premises in St. Vincent Street in the modern city center before relocating again toward the end of the century to the Universities of Glasgow and Strathclyde.) Despite its relatively high price of twelve shillings, six thousand copies of the book were sold within ten weeks and twenty thousand within a year. Chalmers's fame spread rapidly; he was soon preaching in London, where "the cream of London society—in hundreds of carriages—flocked to hear him," while arrangements were set on foot for a 500-page volume of his *Tron Church Sermons* to be put out by the prominent London publishing firm of Longman.[119] He was also already being published in Holland in Dutch translation and was soon to be published in France and Germany in French and German translations. In 1819, however, the by then celebrated Chalmers suggested to his friend and admirer William Collins that he undertake to be the primary publisher of his work, starting with a volume inspired by Chalmers's experience as minister of a parish church in one of Glasgow's poorest districts, to which, with the strong encouragement of Collins, he had voluntarily translated from the upscale Tron Church. As what amounted to a condition of this arrangement, Collins was to take on Charles Chalmers, Chalmers's younger brother, who had great difficulty settling down, as a partner. The house of Collins thus started life as Chalmers and Collins, with William Collins in charge of the publishing side of the business and Charles Chalmers in charge of the printing and bookselling side. (The well-stocked bookshop was located in Wilson Street in the old merchant city section, whereas a small printing works had been set up, with financial assistance from Thomas Chalmers and the family of Collins's wife, Jane Barclay, in nearby Candleriggs.)

In September 1819, the first part of Chalmers's *The Christian and Civic Economy of Large Towns* was published by "Chalmers and Collins, Booksellers and Stationers," at a cost of one shilling. By 1823 the complete work had appeared in three volumes.[120] Additional works by Chalmers came out in rapid succession: *Application of Christianity to the Commercial and Ordinary Affairs of Life* (1820); *The Importance of Civil Government to Society and the Duty of Christians in regard to it* (1820); *Scripture References, designed for the use of Parents, Teachers and private Christians* (1821, originally published by John Smith in 1817); and *A Series of Discourses on the Christian Revelation* (1822, originally published by Smith in 1817).[121] Other works put out at this time also reflect the religious orientation and commitment of the publishers. These included *The Christian Philosopher* (1823) by the Dundee-born science teacher Thomas Dick and *A Practical Review of the Prevailing System of Professed Christians in the Higher and Middle Classes in This Country Contrasted with Real Christianity* by William Wilberforce, the enormously popular evangelical Christian MP responsible for the Slave Trade Act of 1807 (which put an end to the British slave trade) and the Abolition of Slavery Act of 1833 (which ended slavery itself throughout the British Empire). The year 1822 saw the inauguration of the moderately priced "Select Library of Christian Authors," which by 1829 was made up of about fifty consistently popular works of divinity, with prefaces by modern writers, such as Chalmers himself, who provided the preface for Thomas à Kempis's *The Imitation of Christ*, and Wilberforce, who provided the preface for a new edition in 1824 of Scots-born Princeton President John Witherspoon's posthumously published (1804) *Treatises on Justification and Regeneration*.

From the outset, Collins was also deeply engaged in publishing in the field of education, both moral and practical. A first schoolbook, *A System of Commercial Arithmetic for Use in Schools and Private Families*, appeared in 1821. By 1825 the series "Select Christian Biography, Intended for Youth" included over fifty titles, among them works by or adapted from Chalmers, as well as now forgotten moral tales, such as *Pious Grandson, The History of James Anderson* or *The Widow of Rosenheath, a Lesson of Piety*. Dictionaries were also featured, beginning with a Greek–English dictionary, in collaboration with Smith, Elder, in 1826.

In 1826 the firm of Chalmers and Collins began to encounter financial difficulties and clearly did not escape the crisis that affected others in the bookselling and publishing trades around this time, most notably Constable—though it is possible that, as Collins alleged, the difficulties sprang from Charles Chalmers's poor management of the bookselling side or, as Charles Chalmers alleged, from Collins's "venturesomeness" on the publishing side. Whatever the cause, Charles was so alarmed at the prospect of the Chalmers's investments in the firm being swept away in a grand insolvency that, without consulting his brother, by then a professor at the University of St. Andrews, he proposed an immediate dissolution of the partnership. Collins accepted the proposal and with the help of loans and promises from his brothers-in-law succeeded in weathering the storm. The Chalmers–Collins partnership of six and a half years thus came to an end and Collins became master of his own publishing firm.[122]

Nevertheless, despite ups and downs, the close friendship of Thomas Chalmers and William Collins endured and Collins continued to publish the writings of his now internationally celebrated friend after the breakup of the partnership with Charles and until Chalmers definitively defected to the Edinburgh publisher Oliver and Boyd in 1846, a year before his death. *The*

Supreme Importance of a Right Moral to a Right Economic State of the Community appeared in 1831; *Political Economy in Connection with the Moral State and Moral Prospects of Society* in 1832; *Tracts of Pauperism* the following year; the massive 368-page *On the Sufficiency of the Parochial System, without a Poor Rate, for the Right Management of the Poor* in 1841; and *The Collected Works of Thomas Chalmers* in 25 volumes over five years from 1836 to 1841. And Collins continued to focus, in general, on religion and education. In 1828 he published *The Christian Poet*, an anthology edited by the Scottish hymnodist and poet James Montgomery, which sold 2,000 copies within a couple of months and then went into several editions, in different formats, at prices ranging from four shillings to ten shillings and sixpence. Though many of the poems anthologized and arranged in chronological order in this volume are by authors long forgotten, a fair number are by authors who are part of the English literary canon: Chaucer and John Gower for the fourteenth century; John Skelton and Sir Thomas More for the fifteenth to sixteenth centuries; Wyatt and Spenser for the sixteenth century; Donne, Shakespeare, Ben Jonson, and William Drummond for the sixteenth to seventeenth centuries; George Herbert, Robert Herrick, Milton, Bunyan, and Dryden for the seventeenth century; Pope and Chatterton for the eighteenth; and Byron for the nineteenth. In 1841 a license to print the New Testament was obtained and by 1842 Collins was printing complete Bibles. Forty thousand subscribers signed up for an edition of the *Select Practical Writings of John Knox* (the leader of the Reformation in Scotland) that appeared in 1845.

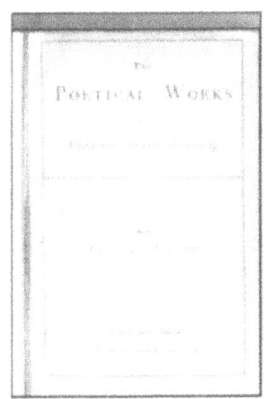

On the death of William Collins, Senior in 1853, his son, also William Collins, a partner in the firm since 1843, formally took over the running of it. Like his father, William Collins II was a businessman, a devout Christian with a deep Christian concern for the material and, above all, moral and spiritual condition of the dangerously neglected poor and working class, and a committed member of the Temperance movement. William Collins II was elected Lord Provost (i.e., Lord Mayor) of Glasgow in 1877 and knighted in 1881. Under his management, Collins moved into the area of scientific encyclopedias and atlases and, in general, concentrated more and more on educational publications. The firm became publisher to the Scottish School Book Association and the Irish National Schools, with more than two million schoolbooks shipped to Ireland between 1853 and 1863. A. M. Trotter's *A Manual of English Grammar* (1873) sold more than half a million copies. By 1862 the company was also selling some three hundred thousand Bibles annually. In 1871, Collins took over the Popular Poets series from the failing London company of Edward Moxon, a friend of Charles Lamb, a poet himself, and a publisher of Wordsworth, Shelley, and Tennyson. Nineteen volumes appeared under the series title "The Grosvenor Poets" at the fairly modest price of 3s 6d for cloth-bound and 7s 6d for leather- bound copies. Among the poets in the series were Burns, Byron, Coleridge, Cowper, Goldsmith, Longfellow, Milton, Moore, Pope, Swift, Shakespeare, Thomson, Wordsworth, and the then immensely popular woman writer Felicia Hemans, who had been one of John Murray's authors in the 1820s.

Under William Collins II, the firm expanded its outreach, opening markets in Canada, Australia, New Zealand, India, and Africa. By the mid-1870s, over 900 titles were being published annually and, by 1879, the annual output of books came to about two million. William Collins III, who succeeded his father as head of the firm after the latter's death in 1895, overhauled and modernized the printing facilities in Glasgow, began to exploit the South American market, set up a new warehouse in Sydney and a William Collins Company office in New York,[123] and—not the least of his achievements—initiated in 1903, three years before his death, the extraordinarily successful Collins Handy Illustrated Pocket Novels series, the only such series at the time to be fully illustrated. Shortly thereafter the series' rather unwieldy title was altered to Collins Illustrated Pocket Classics, which better reflected the categories of works to be represented: not only "Fiction," but "Poetry and Belles-Lettres," "History, Travel, Biography," and "Young People." "The size is small, 6 ¼ ins. by 4 ins.," as the advance notices put it, "the type is bold and well-leaded; the half-tone illustrations are from original drawings and many in number; the price"—at one shilling initially—"is low." The first ten volumes included works by Dickens, Scott, George Eliot, Charles Kingsley, and Charlotte Brontë, and over 80,000 copies were sold in the first six months. By 1908 there were 100 titles in the series, almost all of works still regarded as classics of English literature, and most of them dating from the nineteenth century,[124] and by the 1920s the number of titles had reached more than 300 with the addition of works by canonical writers, such as Pepys and Defoe; American writers, such as Herman Melville and Mark Twain; more recent British writers, such as Walter de la Mare, Thomas Hardy, Robert Louis Stevenson, H. G. Wells, and Oscar Wilde; and a few foreign authors, such as Gustave Flaubert, Anatole France, and Lev Tolstoy. New series were also introduced: the Sevenpenny series of previously published works by living writers in 1907, with the first volume appearing three days after the first volume of the similarly titled series put out by Nelson; the Penny Library series for schools, which included Swift's *Gulliver's Travels* and Kingsley's *The Water Babies*; and the Novel Library, the books in which ranged from thrillers to Galsworthy's *Forsyte* novels and various works by Somerset Maugham (both by arrangement with the original publisher Heinemann). And beyond the series for which Collins was best known a few new writers were recruited: Victoria Sackville-West, John Middleton Murry, Rosamond Lehmann, John Masefield, and for the detective novels that brought in substantial profits, Agatha Christie.

In sum, the contribution of Collins, like that of Nelson and Blackie, lay chiefly in the popularizing of established literary classics. The firm was less prominent as a discoverer and promoter of original new writers.

Blackie and Son (Glasgow) 1831

This firm has a complicated early history. John Blackie, the founder, born in Glasgow in 1781, was sent out to work in the tobacco trade at the age of six, but as that business, which had been booming in Glasgow in previous decades, had slumped as a result of the American war, the young Blackie shifted, at age eleven, to the seemingly more promising handloom weaver's trade. Perhaps because the weavers' trade in turn came under threat, in this case from mechanization, John Blackie left it in 1805, after his marriage and the birth of his first son, John, and found employment with a company of booksellers, A. and W. D. Brownlie. Bookselling in the Scottish countryside at that time often took the form of soliciting subscriptions for books and delivering them in parts. "Except in the larger towns, bookshops were rare—almost unknown—in 1800," Agnes A. C. Blackie explains in her book on the company, published in 1959. "In the country and the smaller towns people were largely dependent on the issue of books in paper bound sections called *numbers*, sold by subscription, and delivered to subscribers section by section. As the sections were moderately priced, and could be paid for one by one, the *numbers* trade also served to put books within the financial reach of relatively poor people."[125] John Blackie's job with the Brownlies was to travel far and wide across Scotland and Northern England, seeking new subscribers and delivering the sections or *numbers* to existing ones. The lesson was not lost on him when he himself moved into bookselling and then publishing—the two trades being still closely connected, with booksellers themselves, in Scotland especially, and in Glasgow as well as Edinburgh, having reprints made of classic and popular works.[126] The Blackie firm sought to reach out to a wide readership and was a pioneer in the production of inexpensive series. Around 1808, the Brownlies arranged for John Blackie to take over their business, which had run into financial difficulty, and the following year Blackie took two friends in as partners, both of whom had also worked for the Brownlies. As of about 1811, besides selling books, the new firm, known as W. Sommerville, A. Fullarton, and J. Blackie & Co., began publishing its own books, chiefly in the areas of history and religion—for example, a *Narrative of the Political and Military Events of 1815* by James McQueen (1815); a translation from the French of Charles Rollin's still popular and highly regarded 12-volume *Histoire ancienne* of 1730–38 (1826); an English version of George Buchanan's Latin

Rerum Scoticarum Historia of 1582 (1829); Thomas Haweis's three-volume *The Evangelical Expositor, or A Commentary on the Holy Bible* of 1765 (1818), of which several editions for family use were published in 65 to 168 "numbers" ranging in price from sixpence to a shilling each, and of which over 14,000 copies were sold; and the occasional fictional classic with a religious resonance (Bunyan's *The Pilgrim's Progress* [1820–23], Richardson's *Pamela, or Virtue Rewarded* [1820–23]).

Over two decades the firm split up in various ways, essentially into a publishing-and-bookselling branch located in Glasgow and a bookselling-only branch in Edinburgh, until in 1831, five years after Blackie's oldest son, John Blackie Jr., had become a partner, the company was re-established as Blackie & Son, and was totally in the hands of the Blackie family. Another five years later, Blackie's second son, William Graham Blackie—who, besides having been trained as a printer had attended the University of Glasgow and obtained a doctorate at the University of Jena in Germany, and who had taken over the running of the Valleyfield Printing Works in Glasgow, purchased by his father some time before and renamed "W. G. Blackie & Co."—was made a partner in his father's publishing firm, to be joined shortly after, in what was now very much a family affair, by John Blackie's youngest son, Robert, who had a keen interest in book illustration and art. (He had studied under Ingres in Paris.[127]) At a somewhat later date Robert's son also joined the firm. By 1842, John Senior had withdrawn into the background leaving his three sons—John Jr., William Graham, and Robert—virtually in charge of the company. The two still independent firms of Blackie & Son (the publishing house) and W. G. Blackie & Co. (the printer) amalgamated in 1890 as Blackie & Sons, Ltd.

For many years Blackie & Sons published technical and practical works appropriate to the burgeoning industrial economy of Glasgow (*The Engineer and Machinist's Assistant* [1843], *Machinery and Mill Work* [1848], *Railway Machinery* [1851], *The Engineer and Machinist's Drawing Book* [1860], *Steam Engines: A Treatise on Steam Engines and Boilers* [1891]), reference works (*The Imperial Dictionary* [1847–50], *The Imperial Gazeteer* [1855], *The Imperial Atlas* [1859], *The Popular Encyclopaedia* [1841], a seven-volume reprint of the late 1820s American version of the Brockhaus *Konversationslexikon*), and religious books (*The Imperial Family Bible* [1841], *The Imperial Bible Dictionary* [1863]). Scottish writers were represented (Hogg's *Poetical Works* [1838–40], Burns's *Poetical Works* [1838–40]), as were some classics of historiography (Ranke's *Popes of Rome* [1846–47]). All, save the *Encyclopaedia*, were issued in "numbers," at relatively modest prices.[128]

From early on, however, the firm also engaged in publishing selections from the works of ancient, modern, and even contemporary literary writers—though, as might be expected, not all in these categories, especially the last, are still read today. These publications were clearly designed to meet the needs of a modestly educated but expanding reading public. Books, Blackie held, were "instruments of enlightenment."[129] At the suggestion of John Blackie, Jr., who had had a more formal education than the senior partner in the firm and who had strong literary interests, Blackie, Fullarton and Co. of Glasgow and A. Fullarton and Co, booksellers of Edinburgh, came together as early as 1828 to publish a two-volume duodecimo *Casquet of Literary Gems* of about 400 double-column pages each, described in the Preface reassuringly as "a collection of pieces of unequivocal merit and unobjectionable tendency, selected in some cases from rare old writers, but principally from the distinguished authors of the present day." Although some of the authors have remained unidentified or have since been largely forgotten, the contributors included many celebrated names: Among them, in the first volume alone, the Scottish woman poet Joanna Baillie, Byron, Thomas Campbell, John Clare, Coleridge, William Cowper, the sixteenth- and seventeenth-century Scottish poets Drummond of Hawthornden and William Dunbar, Dryden, John Galt, Hazlitt, Robert Herrick, Thomas Heywood, Thomas Hood, David Hume, Leigh Hunt, Washington Irving, Isaac D'Israeli, Keats, Charles Lamb, Andrew Marvell, Charles Maturin, and Milton. The collection was edited by one Alex Whitelaw, whom Blackie later employed again to prepare a four-volume "continuation of the *Casquet of Literary Gems*," entitled *The Republic of Letters* (1832) and, a few years later, *A Book of Scottish Song* (1843) and *The Book of Scottish Ballads* (1845). Enhanced by illustrations based on the work of David

Scott, a notable Scottish painter of the time, the relatively inexpensive *Casquet of Literary Gems* went through several new and expanded editions and continued to be published into the 1870s and 1880s.[130] The range of writers was further extended in these later selections to include still more standard writers (Boswell, Chaucer, Congreve, Defoe, Spenser, Sterne, Swift); a fair number of writers still living or only recently deceased (George Borrow, Samuel Butler, Dickens, Kingsley, Bulwer-Lytton, Coventry Patmore, Swinburne, Tennyson, Trollope); several contemporary Americans (Louisa May Alcott, Emerson, Hawthorne, Oliver Wendell Holmes, Longfellow); along with a sprinkling of writers in translation: ancient, modern, and still living (Plato, Dante, Cervantes, Victor Hugo, Turgenev).

The Blackies continued the policy of publishing inexpensive popular editions of works of recognized literary merit right into the twentieth century: "Blackie's English Classics" (early 1890s to 1910) with individual volumes devoted to Bacon, Browning, Goldsmith, Gray, Longfellow, Milton, Pope, Spenser, and Tennyson among others; the expanded *Casquet of Literature: A Selection in Poetry and Prose from the Works of the Most Admired Authors*, six vols. 1874; *The Casquet Library of English Pastorals*, 1895; *The Casquet Library of Lyric Poetry (1500–1700)*, 1897; *The Casquet Library of English Satire*, 1906. Many texts from these collections were later re-edited and reissued in the so-called War-

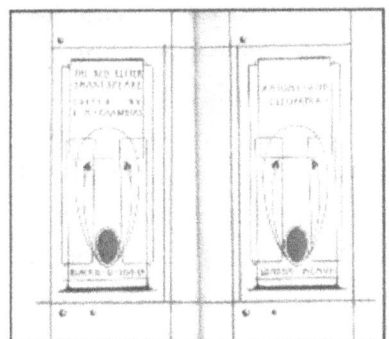

wick Library of English Literature, Blackie's English Texts, Blackie's Latin Texts, Blackie's Longer French Texts, The Wallet Library (in 32mo, featuring a wide range of works by—among others—Bacon, Blake, Byron, Carlyle, Coleridge, De Quincey, Emerson, Hazlitt, Herrick, Lamb, Landor, Montaigne, Milton, Ruskin, and Thoreau, along with More's *Utopia*, and St. Augustine's *Confessions*). In addition, responding to the Education Acts of 1870 and 1872, which made education compulsory from age five to age thirteen, the company put out many series, both entertaining and instructive, designed especially with the education of the young in mind and as "rewards" for "punctual attendance" or "good work and conduct." Blackie's School and Home Library, renamed The Library of Famous Books, featured works not only by well-known authors of children's books—Louisa May Alcott, R. M. Ballantyne, Lewis Carroll, Susan Coolidge, Anna Sewell—but works by standard authors, such as Bunyan, Dickens, Goldsmith, Hawthorne, Scott, Swift, and Robert Louis Stevenson. The company issued catalogues devoted to "Books for younger children and primary school libraries" or "Educational Works specially adapted for elementary and higher schools" (1885).

Blackie, which established an office in London in 1837, and branches in India, Australia, Canada, and for a time New York, thus did a great deal to make the great classics of English literature and some foreign language classics, as well as a fair number of contemporary works, easily accessible to a broad general public. In this respect the company was certainly following the traditional Scottish objective of education for all—spreading the word—as another Glasgow publisher, Collins, and the Edinburgh publisher Thomas Nelson also did, while at the same time pursuing the no-less-characteristic Scottish goal of legitimate financial profit.[131] The company motto, "Lucem libris disseminamus," was entirely appropriate. None of the Blackies seems, however, to have sought out or entertained close social relations with writers, as Constable, Murray, Macmillan, Strahan, and George Murray Smith of Smith, Elder and Co. did, or to have been sought out by them, though the company did use the services of living writers to introduce the works of standard authors (e.g., the novelist George Gissing for the 1901–2 fifteen-volume "Imperial Edition" of the *Works of Charles Dickens*, or the poet Alice Meynell for many of the Blackie Red Letter poets).

In one respect in particular, however, the firm was a remarkable and admirable innovator. In 1893 Talwin Morris was hired as art director and chief book designer— making Blackie perhaps the first publisher to employ a truly gifted and already fairly  well-known artist in such a capacity. Talwin Morris quickly established contact with the artists of the lively, avant-garde Glasgow School and, in particular, with Charles Rennie Mackintosh, whom he introduced to Walter Blackie in 1902, thus preparing the way for Blackie's commissioning Mackintosh to design a house for him— the stunningly beautiful Hill House (now the property of the National Trust for Scotland), just outside Helensburgh, a resort town about twenty miles down the Clyde from Glasgow. Great distinction was brought to Blackie's publications at this time by Talwin Morris's striking *art nouveau* designs for the bindings, title pages, and endpapers of many of the firm's products, including:

- practical or technical works, such as *Modern House Construction* (1898); *The Modern Carpenter and Joiner* (1902); *The Horse: Its Treatment in Health and Disease* (1906); *The Modern Baker, Confectioner and Caterer* (1907); or *Modern Power Generators* (1908)[132]
- children's books: The Crown Series of works by Harriet Beecher Stowe and Fenimore Cooper, among others; Stories Old and New, a series intended for children between the ages of 6 and 8 and 7 and 9 and including works by the brothers Grimm, Hawthorne, Defoe, and Swift; Little French Classics with short works by Alexandre Dumas, Alphonse de Lamartine, Prosper Mérimée, and Alfred de Vigny, as well as a volume of poems
- books for older schoolchildren: Longer French Texts, with volumes devoted to Chateaubriand, Baudelaire and Nodier; a French Plays Series, with works by Molière, Labiche, and others; Little German Classics, with Heine's *Harzreise* and Schiller's *Der Neffe als Onkel*; The Plain-Text Poets with "Shorter Poems" by Milton and Longfellow's *The Song of Hiawatha*

- the Sixpenny Classics and the popular and modestly priced Red Letter series, directed toward a larger reading public and including the Red Letter Shakespeare, and the Red Letter Poets, each volume of the latter being devoted to the work of a major modern poet, such as Matthew Arnold, Elizabeth Barrett Browning, Robert Browning, Longfellow, Christina Rossetti, Shelley, or Tennyson.

W. & R. Chambers (Edinburgh) 1832

The extraordinarily successful firm of W. & R. Chambers was founded by two brothers—William (b. 1800) and Robert (b. 1802)—the sons of a moderately well-off cotton producer in the southern Scottish town of Peebles, employing at one time as many as a hundred individual handloom weavers. Both boys received a basic primary education at the local school, enhanced by input from the local bookseller, Alexander ("Sandy," as the boys called him) Elder, "a decent man [...] enterprising and enlightened beyond the common range of booksellers in small country towns." Elder had opened a circulating library, which was patronized by the boys' father James Chambers, and thanks to which they got to "read a considerable number of the classics of English literature" and "were made familiar," in particular, "with the comicalities of Gulliver, Don Quixote, and Peregrine Pickle," with "Pope's translation of the Iliad," with Fielding and Sterne, and with the fourth edition of the *Encyclopaedia Britannica*, purchased from Elder's library by their father. William later paid generous tribute, in his *Memoir of Robert Chambers* published after Robert's death in 1872, to the boys' "friend Alexander Elder," "in whom there was certainly something considerably superior to the common book-trader" and whose "catalogue included several books striking far above the common taste."[133] With the advent of steam looms in the manufacture of cotton James Chambers's business fell upon hard times, however, and in 1813 the family had to give up its home and move to Edinburgh, where William was apprenticed to an Edinburgh bookseller for five years at four shillings a week.

Robert was able to continue his formal education for a bit, in the hope that he might attend the university and enter the ministry. A further deterioration in the family fortunes, however, put an end, in 1816, to Robert's schooling also. The younger Chambers undertook some private tutoring and served for a time as a junior clerk in commercial houses until, in 1818, at the age of sixteen, following his brother's advice, he opened a bookstall for second-hand books on Leith Walk, the thoroughfare leading down from Edinburgh to the port at Leith. His stock consisted of the family book collection and his own schoolbooks. An expert calligrapher, he was able to augment the slim takings from his book sales by producing handwritten documents for special occasions, and a few years later he was to make a friend and ally of Walter Scott on presenting him, at the suggestion of John Constable, with a beautifully handwritten anthology of songs from *The Lady of the Lake*. On the occasion of George IV's visit to Scotland, Scott obtained for Robert the assignment of writing out the Royal Society of Edinburgh's address to His Majesty, for which he was, in Robert's own words, "handsomely paid."[134]

A year after Robert opened his stall on Leith Walk, William, having completed his apprenticeship, did likewise, except that, thanks to a grant of ten pounds' worth of books on credit, he focused on selling new books from the stall he had built himself. From the start he chose to sell books bound in inexpensive boards rather than leather or even cloth. Soon he was buying books in sheets, which he himself folded, sewed, and bound in boards "thereby saving on an average threepence to fourpence a volume." Next he managed to acquire for three pounds an old hand press and a bundle of "dreadfully old and worn" types. With these he was able to undertake odd printing jobs and soon afterward produced an edition of 750 copies, "small size, of the Songs of Robert Burns," bound "with my own hands [...] in boards, with a coloured wrapper." All copies were sold, Chambers later reported, clearing a profit of nine pounds.[135] Soon afterward, in 1822, the twenty-year-old Robert wrote and brother William printed and published a volume—*Illustrations of the Author of Waverley*—purportedly describing the real individuals on whom many of Walter Scott's characters were based. Received by the public, according to the author, "with some degree of encouragement" [136] this early work had a second edition in 1825, thanks to the striking success of the author's next book, *Traditions of Edinburgh* (1825, originally published and sold in parts), which led Scott to express "astonishment as to where the boy got all the information" and shortly afterwards to call on the young writer with "sixteen folio pages, in his usual close handwriting, and containing all the reminiscences he could at the time summon up of old persons and things in Edinburgh."[137] The association developed over time into a friendship and the mature and celebrated Scott let himself be accompanied by the up-and-coming Chambers on his walks home from Parliament House in Edinburgh.

In 1823, the brothers' stock had increased enough to allow them to move to more substantial quarters in Edinburgh proper. Robert built on the success of *Traditions of Edinburgh* by composing a number of other books on Scottish subjects: *Popular Rhymes of Scotland* (1826) and, as volumes in Constable's Miscellany series, a *History of the Rebellion of 1745* (1828), followed by his *History of the Rebellions in Scotland from 1638 till 1660* (also 1828) and *History of the Rebellions in Scotland in 1689 and 1715* (1829). Together the brothers produced a *Gazeteer of Scotland* (1832). It was also in 1832 that the Chambers brothers embarked on their as-yet most significant venture.

This was *Chambers' Edinburgh Journal*, a low-price weekly periodical, consisting of eight folio pages (later reduced, for convenience, to royal octavo) printed in three columns each and priced at three-halfpence for each issue. The aim of the new journal, which was William's idea and of which he was to be the managing editor, while the at-first skeptical and reluctant Robert, serving (as of the fourteenth number) as the literary editor, was expected to offer instructive and entertaining essays and articles on a wide range of topics—literature, science, government, trade and commerce, education, agriculture, industry—in a form accessible to the mass readership believed to have been created by new legislation affecting public education. At the same time, by including fiction and avoiding particular political and religious agendas, the brothers hoped to distinguish their publication from the—so they claimed—more one-sidedly "edifying" journals that had preceded theirs.

The first number, issued on February 4, 1832, contained an opening address that is worth quoting at some length inasmuch as it outlines clearly the brothers' motivations. That there was also no doubt an unspoken aim of tapping into a potentially lucrative market need not invalidate the nobler motivations presented in the address:

> The principle by which I have been actuated, is to take advantage of the universal appetite for instruction which at present exists; to supply to that appetite food of the best kind, in such form and at such price as must suit the convenience of every man in the British dominions. Every Saturday, when the poorest labourer in the country draws his humble earnings, he shall have it in his power to purchase with an insignificant portion of that humble sum, a meal of healthful, useful, and agreeable mental instruction. [. . .] It may perhaps be considered an invidious remark when I state as my humble conviction, that the people of Great Britain and Ireland have never yet been properly cared for, in the way of presenting knowledge under its most cheering and captivating aspect, to their immediate observation. The scheme of diffusing knowledge has certainly been more than once attempted.
> [. . .] Yet the great end has not been gained. The dearth of the publications, official inflexibility, and above all the plan of attaching the interests of political or ecclesiastical parties to the course of instruction of reading, have separately or conjunctly circumscribed the limits of the operation; so that the world, on the whole, is but little the wiser with all the attempts that have been made. [. . .] Carefully eschewing the errors into which these praiseworthy associations have fallen. I take a course altogether novel. Whatever may be my political principles, neither these nor any other which would be destructive of my present views, shall ever mingle in my observations on the arrangements of civil society.[138]

Within a few days, William relates, the magazine had sold thiry thousand copies in Scotland alone and "shortly afterwards, when copies were assigned to an agent in London, [. . .] the sale rose to upwards of fifty thousand, at which it long remained. Some years afterwards, the circulation exceeded eighty thousand."[139] In his *Memoir of Robert Chambers*, William cites with pride a letter, dated 27 October 1832, which Robert received from a correspondent living in England and which presents a no doubt somewhat romanticized picture of the extraordinary success of the *Journal*: "My wife, who has just returned from Scotland, says that your *Journal* is very popular among her native hills of Galloway. The shepherds, who are scattered there at the rate of one to every four miles square, read it constantly, and they circulate it in this way: the first shepherd who gets it reads it, and at an understood hour places it under a stone on a certain hill-top; then shepherd the second in his own time finds it, reads it, and carries it to another hill, where it is found like Ossian's chief under its own grey stone by shepherd the third, and so it passes on its way, scattering information over the land."[140] William was too smart, however, and too authentically committed to his project of raising the cultural and intellectual level of the working masses not to grasp the real character of the journal's popularity. "This paper is read, we believe," he admitted in the issue of 25 January, 1840, "by a class who may be called the *élite* of the labouring community; those who think, conduct themselves respectably, and are anxious to improve their circumstances by judicious means. But below this worthy order of men, our work, except in a few particular cases, does not go. A fatal mistake is committed in the popular notion that the lower classes read. There is, unfortunately, a vast substratum in society, where the printing-press has not yet unfolded her treasures."[141] About the *Journal*'s success in the higher ranks of society, in contrast, there is little doubt. It was read and appreciated by writers of distinction, such as Charlotte Brontë, Leigh Hunt, Thomas De Quincey, and Harriet Martineau.[142]

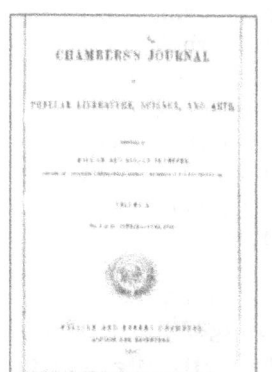

In 1854 the title of the journal was changed to *Chambers's Journal of Popular Literature, Science, and Art* and in 1899 to *Chambers's Journal*, as which it survived until 1956. Its basic character did not change, however, and its final "passing" was "regretted" in the London *Times* "as that of a distinctive journal which has played a memorable part in the history of periodical literature for more than 120 years."[143]

During the early years, in addition to many essays by Robert, the *Journal* published work by Maria Edgeworth, John Galt, and the poet Thomas Hood. Though most of the innumerable nineteenth-century contributors of novels and short stories are almost completely forgotten today, including the extraordinarily productive and popular James Payn (1830–98), who served as editor of the *Journal* from 1860 to 1875, as literary adviser to the firm of Smith, Elder & Co., and as editor of that company's *Cornhill Magazine* as of 1883, and who is represented in the *Journal* between 1854 and 1874 by no fewer than seventeen novels in installments, in addition to countless short stories,[144] *Chambers's* did publish literary fiction by a number of writers still remembered and occasionally read today, such as Leslie Stephen (three short stories in 1866), Margaret Oliphant (*A House Divided Against Itself*, in forty-eight installments [1885]), the astonishingly prolific Walter Besant (*The Ivory Gate*, in thirty-nine installments [1892] and *The Master Craftsman*, in twenty-six installments [1896]), and John Buchan (*John Burnett of Barns: A Romance*, in twenty-six installments [1897–98]). In addition, George Meredith's first published work, the poem "Chillianwallah" appeared in 1849, Thomas Hardy's "How I Built Myself a House" in 1865, and Arthur Conan Doyle's "The Mystery of Sasassa Valley" in 1879, while the author was still a medical student at Edinburgh University.

It does appear that while Robert strongly supported the journal's literary selections and the fictional writings and editorial policies of James Payn in particular, he had to defend them against the reservations of William, who remained faithful to his original goals and complained of the levity of the popular literature appearing in the journal. Though Payn's serialized novel *The Family Scapegrace* (1861), for instance, was apparently well received by the journal's readers and had been read in advance and approved by Robert, William, as Payn himself reports, "objected to it on the ground of its 'lightness.' He would have preferred the subject of wild beasts to have been more 'intelligently treated'; their various habitats to be described, and some sort of moral to be deduced from them."[145]

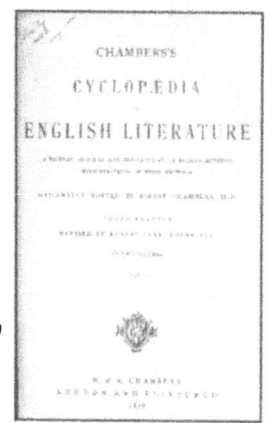

William's view of his role as a publisher was in fact never abandoned. In 1833–35, as the *Journal* was taking off, the brothers launched another project. *Information for the People*—issued in one hundred fortnightly parts priced at three-halfpence each and then published as a volume in 1835—was intended, in the words of the preface to the 1842 edition, "to place a work of the character of an encyclopedia *really* within the reach of the working-classes and those next above them" while selecting "only the subjects on which it is important that the classes in question should be informed." In accessible language free of technical detail, the articles were to cover "the most important branches of science, physical, mathematical, and moral, natural history, political history, geography, and literature." In this way, "all is given which, if studied and received into the mind, would make an individual of those classes a *well-informed man*."[146] By 1874–75 the work had gone through five editions with more than 170,000 copies sold and a French translation issued in Paris.

The success of *Information for the People* encouraged the Chambers brothers to pursue similar projects. In 1835 a still larger project was announced—Chambers's Educational Course, a series of treatises and schoolbooks, ultimately numbering 306 parts, issued at various intervals until 1896. The series largely reflected Scottish educational practice; in fact, many of the volumes were written by teachers in Scottish schools. It was one of the first schoolbook series to include the physical sciences and maps. As a contemporary noted in 1873, "this series begins with a three-halfpenny infant primer, and goes onward through a whole library of grammars, dictionaries, histories, scientific, and all primary class books, and cheap editions of standard foreign and classical authors, until it culminates in a popular 'Encyclopaedia in ten thick volumes.'"[147] Anticipating Blackie, Collins, and Nelson, the brothers launched their "People's Editions" of standard authors in 1838; by 1840 the series already numbered thirty-two volumes of inexpensive reprints, including works by Addison, Bacon, Burns, Crabbe, Defoe, Franklin, Goldsmith, Locke, Allan Ramsey, Scott, and Smollett. This was followed in 1842–43 by a *Cyclopaedia of English Literature: A History, Critical and Biographical, of British Authors, in All Departments of Literature, Illustrated by Specimens of Their Writings*, published in eighty-six weekly parts at the by then expected price of three-halfpence each, and in 1844 as a two- volume set in royal octavo. Largely the work of Robert Chambers but inspired by William's goal of "improvement," the *Cyclopaedia* effectively wove a carefully prepared set of "extracts from our national authors" into a history of British literature. Within a few years, 130,000 copies had been sold and four editions had been put out by the end of the century, with a fifth in 1910, to which well-known writers like George Saintsbury and Andrew Lang contributed. New editions continued to be put out until 1938.

Finally, between 1860 and 1868 the brothers produced what they called their "crowning achievement in cheap and instructive literature." This was *Chambers's Encyclopaedia: A Dictionary of Useful Knowledge*, originally published in 520 weekly numbers at the usual three-halfpence each and then as a 10-volume reference work. Based on the celebrated German *Brockhaus Konversations-Lexikon* (1838–41), which was adapted to rather than translated for English-speaking users, this work again aimed to avoid elaborate, highly technical treatises on various topics and to provide instead readily accessible and relatively short entries suitable for the general reader. It turned out to be a great success, as well as a highly profitable venture. A revised edition appeared in 1888–92, with further new and revised editions until 1935. A completely reconceived version came out shortly after the end of World War II, with a different publisher (George Newnes, by arrangement with the Chambers company).

Although both Chambers brothers produced books of their own and each had his own interests and inclinations—Robert's being more literary and historical, William's more scientific and practical—their close partnership, to which William's *Memoir* of the life of his brother bears eloquent witness, facilitated a broadly conceived pursuit of the goal of intellectual and moral improvement originally set forth by William. At the same time, sound business practices and decisions ensured handsome profits and the continued viability of the company. Like Collins and Nelson, W. & R. Chambers did more to spread knowledge and understanding of the literary canon than, like Murray and Smith and Elder, to promote new literary talents.

Macmillan (Cambridge and London) 1843

One of the largest and most influential publishing houses in the English-speaking world was founded by two brothers born into a deeply religious crofting family—on the mountainous Isle of Arran in the Firth of Clyde in the case of Daniel (1813–57), the elder brother, and in the small Ayrshire port town of Irvine across the Firth on the mainland in the case of Alexander (1818–96), the younger. Their father, who continued to keep a few cows and to cultivate some acres of land after the move to Irvine, also worked as a carter carrying coal from the nearby pits to the harbor at Irvine. He died in 1823 and his many children were raised by their mother, Katherine Crawford, the daughter of a slightly better-off farmer on Arran, and by their oldest brother, a schoolmaster of twenty-five at the time of their father's death. In the new family circumstances, Daniel had to give up schooling and start earning a living. He was indentured for a period of seven years to a bookseller in Irvine at a salary of eighteen pence a week, serving so well that at the age of fifteen he was left in charge of the shop while his master went to London on business. In 1831, his apprenticeship having ended, he went to work first for a bookseller in Stirling and then for a bookseller in Glasgow, who also left him in charge while on a trip to London and rewarded him for his diligence and sound judgment with a substantial bonus. This allowed him to imagine new ventures of his own, but the first signs of the tuberculosis that was to kill him at a fairly young age forced him to return to Irvine to be taken care of by his mother. Once over the worst of his illness, he made his way back to London to look for work there. During his time In Glasgow he had made the acquaintance of James

MacLehose, who was to be the founder, in the late 1830s, of the prominent Glasgow bookselling and subsequently printing and publishing firm that still bears his name. MacLehose had gone to London as an assistant in Seeley's Fleet Street bookstore and shared his lodgings with Daniel while the younger man desperately looked for a job with various London publishers and booksellers. In the end, he had to accept a position in Cambridge but returned to Scotland soon after the death of his mother and would have settled for a position as shopman to a stationer in Leith had MacLehose not contrived to find a position for him at the Fleet Street bookstore where he himself had been employed.[148] In 1839, Daniel persuaded Seeley's to take on his brother Alexander also. Alexander had worked at various poorly paid occupations and had even sailed to America in the hope of improving his lot. Less well read than his brother, he set out to remedy that situation on joining Seeley's, becoming a keen fan of Shelley in particular. He drew up a selection of poems or parts of poems that particularly pleased him, added a short biographical sketch, and succeeded in having the little volume published anonymously by George Bell, who had just opened shop in 1839, first in Bouverie Street and then, the following year, in Fleet Street, not far from Seeley's.

By 1843 the brothers felt they had acquired sufficient experience—Daniel was thirty, Alexander twenty-five—to open a bookselling business of their own in Aldersgate Street, where the rent was affordable. As this was not the best location for a bookstore, however, when an opportunity arose later that year to acquire a bookseller's business in Cambridge, the brothers seized it, thanks to the financial assistance of Julius Hare, the well-to-do, cultured Archdeacon of Lewes in Sussex, with whom they had established friendly relations through their enthusiastic interest in writings on religious topics, in particular those of Archdeacon Hare's friend F. D. Maurice, the author of *The Kingdom of Christ* (1838) and one of the founders of Christian Socialism. Among the earliest of the brothers' publications as they began gradually to extend their activities from bookselling to publishing was a reprint in 1844 of William Law's critical *Remarks* of 1724 on Mandeville's celebrated *Fable of the Bees* (1714), with an introduction by Maurice. The Macmillans remained devout Christians all their lives and Maurice, whom they termed their "Prophet," remained throughout the years one of their most frequently published authors. As he had studied at Cambridge, it was probably he who introduced a number of Cambridge scholars to the brothers when they first started out in the little university city. In any case, the Macmilllan bookshop in Trinity Street quickly became a haunt of both faculty and students. An upper common room, reserved precisely for the purpose, was soon the scene of lively discussions of philosophy, theology, and social issues among students, faculty, and townspeople visiting the store—discussions in which Daniel and especially Alexander (for Daniel had frequent bouts of illness that required him to leave Cambridge) took part. The list of publications for the 1840s and 50s, in which—a characteristic of so many Scottish publishers—religion, science, Greek and Latin classics, and textbooks for schools predominate, is notable for the number of works authored or edited by fellows of Cambridge colleges.[149]

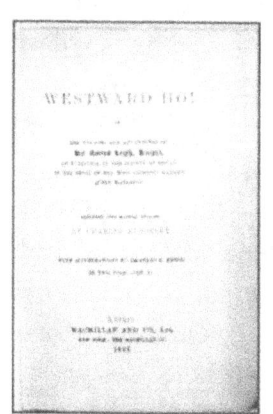

Maurice's greatest contribution to the success of the Macmillans as publishers, however, was bringing to them a former student (Maurice held a position at King's College in London), the Reverend Charles Kingsley, rector of a village in Hampshire. Except for a short pamphlet entitled "Cheap Clothes and Nasty" (1850), an attack on the shocking working conditions in the London tailors' trade, Kingsley's first publication with the brothers was *Phaeton, or Loose Thoughts for Loose Thinkers*, a hundred-page-long philosophical meditation presented in lively, fictional form. The modest octavo volume, put out in 1852, appears to have sold moderately well, because a second edition appeared in 1854—that is, before the enormous success of the author's *Westward Ho!*—and a third in 1858. It was indeed, however, *Westward Ho!* that put Kingsley—and Macmillan—on the map and provided the company with a solid financial foundation. With its idea of a "muscular Christianity" committed to fighting the evils in Victorian society, *Westward*

Ho! turned out to be a bestseller. The original three-decker of 1855, each volume of which was over 300 pages, had a first print-run of 1,250 copies, with a second printing of 750 copies three months later, and a third, of 6,000 copies, in 1857. Between 1861 and 1889 there were fifteen further reprints or new editions, barely two or three years apart. The sixpenny edition of that last year sold 500,000 copies.[150] Kingsley continued to entertain close and friendly relations with Macmillan—"A thousand thanks for your obligingness," he wrote to Alexander in 1856. "You certainly are a most pleasant person to deal with"[151]—and to produce works for the company (about forty in all), among them some that turned out, like *Westward Ho!*, to be bestsellers and a few that are still read and republished in our own time: *Glaucus, Or the Wonders of the Shore* (five editions or reprints between 1855 and 1878), *The Water-Babies* (fourteen editions between 1863 and 1889), *Hypatia* (thirteen editions between 1863 and 1886, with a sixpenny edition in 1889), *Hereward the Wake* (four editions between 1866 and 1889).

Kingsley's most successful works, whatever their underlying theme, took the form of fiction, and although Macmillan continued to publish scholarly books on religion, philosophy, and science, along with educational books and the great texts of classical antiquity, the enormous success of *Westward Ho!* appears to have encouraged the firm to reorient itself toward the hitherto neglected field of fiction. One of the first fictional works to follow Kingsley's was another huge success, Thomas Hughes's *Tom Brown's School Days*, about which the author had told the Macmillans "I'm going to make your fortune,"[152] and which, published anonymously in April 1857, sold 11,000 copies by the end of the year. The turn to fiction coincided with a development contemplated by the brothers for some time and realized shortly after Daniel's death in 1857 from the TB that had plagued him throughout his life, namely, the opening in Henrietta Street, Covent Garden, of a London branch of the company. Though the head office remained in Cambridge for a time, Alexander came to London every Thursday and, following the pattern he and Daniel had set in Cambridge, welcomed his authors, prospective authors, and friends to the Henrietta Street premises for gatherings that came to be known as the "Tobacco Parliaments." Alexander took a keen interest in the work of his writers and they appreciated his engagement and advice. Leading figures in the literary and intellectual world, such as Hughes, Thomas Henry Huxley, Kingsley, Maurice, Francis Turner Palgrave, Coventry Patmore, Herbert Spencer, and Alfred Tennyson ("he smokes like a good Christian," Alexander said approvingly of him[153]), would come together to smoke (for Alexander, it appears, "there was always something orgiastic in the idea of smoking"[154]), take tea and spirits, and discuss the major issues of the day. The result appears to have been a reinforcing of the expansion, already under way, of the firm's range of publications and the launching in November 1859—two months before the *Cornhill* of Smith and Elder—of the first of the monthly shilling magazines. Over the forty-eight years of its existence, *Macmillan's Magazine* hosted—in addition to poetry by Tennyson, Christina Rossetti, Longfellow, George Meredith, and Matthew Arnold, and essays by Arnold, Herbert Spencer, Thomas Henry Huxley, and Harriet Martineau—works of fiction in serial form by Charles Kingsley, Margaret Oliphant, Thomas Hardy, and the American writers Francis Marion Crawford and Henry James. Matthew Arnold and Alexander Macmillan had a particularly close relationship of mutual respect and trust, with well over two dozen volumes of essays and poems by Arnold being published, frequently reprinted, and put out in new editions by the house of Macmillan.[155] Though the Tennyson connection was somewhat less smooth, Tennyson being a notoriously hard bargainer, Alexander was a true admirer of his work. In a letter of January 1884, written on the occasion of a new contract with the poet to Tennyson's wife, Emily, herself a poet, Alexander recounted that "it is just forty years since I first read 'Poems by Alfred Tennyson', and got bitten by a healthy mania from which I have not recovered—and don't want to recover. [. . .] How much I owe to Alfred Tennyson for the increase of ennobling thought & feeling, no one can tell. Now our closer connection will not lessen my desire to repay the debt."[156]

Two years after the first appearance of the company's magazine, Alexander published Palgrave's *Golden Treasury of the Best Songs and Lyrical Poems in the English Language*, which soon became a classic anthology frequently revised (for whatever  reason, Palgrave did not include Blake, Donne, or even Coleridge's "Kubla Kahn" in the original edition) and brought up to date. Cautiously, Alexander limited the first printing, in July 1861, to 1,000 copies, but reprints followed in October, November, and December of the same year, and fourteen further reprints were issued between 1862 and 1883. A new edition with many additions appeared in 1884, to be reprinted every year until 1888.[157] Further editions of this work are still being produced in the twenty-first century.

Hard on the heels of Palgrave's *Golden Treasury* came, in 1862, the Golden Treasury Series of old and new literary classics. The early volumes featured works in prose and verse by Bacon, Bunyan, Cowper, Defoe, Milton, and Matthew Arnold's selections from Byron and Wordsworth; by 1890, the series included over forty authors, including near contemporaries such as Longfellow and Tennyson. A spin-off of the series was Coventry Patmore's *Children's Garland* (1862), a selection of poems for the young by both earlier and fairly recent writers, including Blake, Coleridge, Cowper, Keats, Longfellow, Milton, Scott, Shakespeare, Tennyson, and Wordsworth, as well as some traditional ballads. In 1868 the Globe Editions were initiated, beginning with a Globe Shakespeare, inspired by a nine-volume scholarly edition of the master put out by Macmillan, in collaboration with Cambridge University Press, in 1863–66. Alexander described his intention, at once educational and commercial, in a letter to his Glasgow friend, the printer and publisher James MacLehose:

> I enclose a page for a *Shakespeare*, which I fancy doing in one volume, on tone paper, for 3s. 6d., very nicely bound in Macmillan's choicest cloth binding. The text to be gone over by our Cambridge editors, but done in this edition with an eye to more popular uses than they felt themselves at liberty to consider in their critical and scholarly edition. [...] Your judgment is always as you know precious to me. [...] I want you to tell me, whether you think I have a reasonable chance of selling 50,000 of such a book in three years. For if so, I can do a nice stroke of business. You see it would

be immeasurably the cheapest, most beautiful and handy book that has appeared of *any kind*, except the Bible.[158]

After a slow start in the first weeks, the publication took off and twenty thousand copies were sold in a few months. Alexander lost no time extending the series to a wide range of ancient and modern poets, from Virgil and Horace to Spenser, Burns, Scott, and George Meredith, with most volumes going through multiple reprints.[159]

The year 1878 saw the launch of the English Men of Letters series, a pet project of John Morley, a writer himself and the editor of the *Cornhill* magazine, a leading ifsomewhat maverick liberal in politics, a future MP for Newcastle (1883), Chief Secretary for Ireland under Gladstone (1886), and one of Alexander Macmillan's most trusted readers. The volumes in the first two years of this series included presentations of the life and work of Samuel Johnson by Leslie Stephen, of Shelley by John Addington Symonds, of Thackeray by Anthony Trollope, of Nathaniel Hawthorne by Henry James, and of Hume by Thomas Huxley. Many other writers (among them Burns, Carlyle, Defoe, Gibbon, Goldsmith, Milton, Scott, Spenser) were the subjects of later volumes with thirty-nine in all having been published by the time the first series was closed in 1892. (A second series was begun in 1902.) Morley's rationale for the English Men of Letters series communicates a sense of the social and cultural considerations that, as we have seen, underlay not only other Macmillan series—such as the Golden Treasury, the Globe Library, the Colonial Library, launched in 1886 and designed primarily for the Indian market, and the English Classics series, begun the following year with an edition of Scott's *Marmion* that included an introduction and notes by the editor—but, in all probability, similar collections by other publishing companies with strong Scottish backgrounds, such as Blackie, Collins, and Nelson.

> Our object is—and it is that which in my opinion raises us infinitely above the Athenian level—to bring the Periclean ideals of beauty

and simplicity and cultivation of the mind within the reach of those who do the drudgery and service and rude work of the world. And it can be done—do not let us be afraid—it can be done without in the least degree impairing the skill of our handicraftsmen or the manliness of our national life.[160]

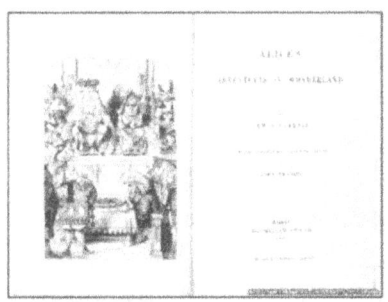

The series' aim, in sum, is to promote the education and cultural improvement of the lower classes without provoking demands for drastic social or political change—indeed, perhaps, as a means of fending off radicalism and undesirable change—while at the same time (though, unlike Alexander himself, Morley does not mention this) achieving substantial sales by addressing a mass market.[161]

All in all, Macmillan did a fine job of making both early and fairly recent English literature—as well as some classic and more modern texts of French literature (Corneille, Daudet, Dumas, Molière, Racine, George Sand, De Tocqueville) and German literature (Goethe, Heine, Klopstock, Schiller, Uhland) in translation—accessible to a broad public. The firm also promoted a number of important contemporary writers, not least the American novelists Francis Marion Crawford and Henry James, the essayist Ralph Waldo Emerson, the essayist and poet Oliver Wendell Homes, Sr., and the poet Henry Wadsworth Longfellow, all of whom are generously represented among the company's authors. (Macmillan had opened a New York branch of the company in 1869.) Tennyson was a friend of Alexander Macmillan and his work figures prominently in the company's lists. Though relations with Lewis Carroll were more complicated, Macmillan brought out *Alice's Adventures in Wonderland* (1866) and *Through the Looking Glass* (1872), both of which went through countless reprints and were also published by Macmillan in French and German translations, as well as the rather less successful *Hunting of the Snark* (1877) and *Sylvie and Bruno* (1889). Between 1862 and 1881 four volumes of poetry by Christina Rossetti appeared. Although George Meredith's novels came out with other publishers, Macmillan brought out three volumes of his poems (1883, 1887, 1888). Walter Pater's *Marius the Epicurean* appeared in 1885. As noted previously, Matthew Arnold was one of Macmillan's most prolific and loyal authors, his work being much admired by Alexander Macmillan personally. "I have read the greater part of your volume through, with care & great admiration," Alexander wrote to "my dear Arnold" on the occasion of the publication of the latter's *New Poems* (1867). "Empedocles is a noble poem. I had only a dim remembrance of it, and thought of it as obscure. I did not find it so this reading. I really think you should succeed."[162] *Essays in Criticism* (1865) was followed by several volumes of Arnold's poems (1867, 1869, 1877) and by his editions of Wordsworth (1874) and Byron (1881), to say nothing of his many essays on issues of culture and education.

Despite hesitations and some early rejections, Macmillan also published Thomas Hardy and Rudyard Kipling in the last decades of the nineteenth century and the first decade of the twentieth. As noted earlier, Hardy's *The Woodlanders* first appeared in serial form in the company's *Magazine* and was then published as a separate volume in 1887. *Wessex Tales* appeared the following year. In 1902, Hardy's contract with Harper & Brothers having run its course, he offered his books to Macmillan "in view of my long personal acquaintance with the members of your firm."[163] In the correspondence that ensued, there was much discussion of putting out inexpensive popular editions of Hardy's works. *A Laodicean* (1903), *Tess of the D'Urbervilles* (1904), *The Dynasts* (1904–08), and *The Mayor of Casterbridge* (1908) soon came out as parts of Hardy's *Complete Works in Prose and Verse* (1903–14). A fair number of stories and poems by Kipling had already been accepted for publication in *Macmillan's Magazine* when the publisher brought out *Plain Tales from the Hills* in 1890. As Kipling quickly became an international success (a French translation of *Kim* appeared in 1901 and Kipling was deeply admired by André Maurois, who translated several of his poems), he was soon being solicited by a range of publishers, including Methuen, Sampson and Lowe, and Scribner's of New York, whose interest in his work he exploited to the full. Macmillan cannot therefore claim to have "discovered" or particularly promoted Kipling. Nevertheless, the company remained one of this author's most constant and reliable publishers. A first edition of *His Private Honour* was brought out by Macmillan in 1891; *Life's Handicap* and *Barrack-Room Ballads* followed in 1893, the *Jungle Book* in 1894, the *Second Jungle Book* in 1895, *Soldiers Three* also in 1895, *Wee Willie Winkie* and *The Light that Failed* in 1896, *Captains Courageous* in 1897, *Stalky & Co.* in 1899, the *Just So Stories* in 1902, and *Puck of Pooks Hill* in 1906. *The Kipling Reader*, a selection of his tales, appeared in 1900, with fourteen reprintings down to 1923— four alone at the end of World War I in 1918–19. In contrast to its ultimately fairly successful dealings with Hardy and Kipling, the Macmillan Company bungled its dealings with George Bernard Shaw and H. G. Wells. Alexander Macmillan followed the advice of the firm's professional readers and rejected the first two submissions by Shaw—the novels *Immaturity* in 1880 and *The Irrational Knot* in 1881— albeit the first was acknowledged by the company's reader, John Morley, to have "a certain quality about it" and to be "undoubtedly clever," while the second was judged to be "clearly the work of a man with a certain originality and courage of mind." A couple of years later Macmillan again declined an opportunity to publish Shaw, this time the novel *Cashel Byron's Profession.* A report dated 22 January 1884 described the work as "by no means without flavor or originality; the writing too is brisk and rapid. But the story is too whimsical

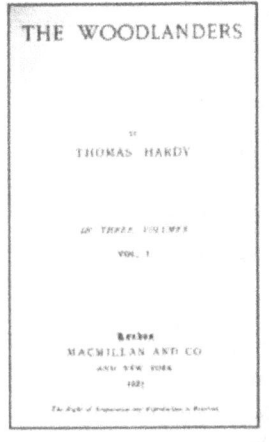

for anything."[164] The manuscript was rejected by other publishers also, except for two small London houses, The Modern Press in 1886 and the Walter Scott Company in 1889.[165] Undeterred, Shaw submitted a fourth work, *An Unsocial Socialist*, to Macmillan in 1885. John Morley's judgment was again mixed, but by no means unfavorable, and worth quoting at some length:

> A curious bit of writing which has appeared in the socialist magazine *Today*, It is a *jeu d'esprit*, or satire, with a good stroke of socialist meaning in it.
>
> The story is designedly paradoxical, absurd, and impossible. [...] But whoever he may be, the author knows how to write; he is pointed, rapid, forcible, sometimes witty, often powerful, and occasionally eloquent. I suppose one must call his book a trifle, but it is a clever trifle. Would it be popular? I half fear that it is too clever for the general. [...] Nor are the pages of socialist irony upon things as they are, and *a priori* demonstrations of the injustice of private property, very attractive to a large public. The present book is Ruskinian doctrine; theories with a whimsical and deliberately extravagant story served up with pungent literary sauce. The result is a dish, which I fancy only the few would relish. On the other hand, the subject is much in vogue [...] and the writer has a telling style of presenting current arguments. I would not prophesy a financial success [...] but the writer, if he is young, is a man to keep one's eye upon.[166]

In rejecting Shaw's submission, Macmillan wrote that the company "would be glad to look at anything else he might write of a more substantial kind." Shaw responded sharply that Macmillan's reader had apparently judged the book trivial and not serious, "perhaps because it was not dull." Moreover, "when one deals with two large questions in a novel, and throws in an epitome of modern German socialism as set forth by Marx as a makeweight, it is rather startling to be met with an implied accusation of triviality." Shaw divined—rightly it would seem—that it was primarily a commercial consideration, namely, the outlook for sales, that had led to his book's being turned down—as Macmillan essentially admitted in a reply to Shaw's response: "What we really doubt is whether the book would find enough readers." To that, in his view, more honest explanation, Shaw again responded courteously: "Surely, out of thirty millions of copyright persons (so to speak) there must be a few thousand who would keep me in bread and cheese for the sake of my story-telling, if you would only let me get at them."[167] Inevitably Macmillan lost Shaw to other publishers and in the end, the only work of his that the company published was a nine-page illustrated article entitled "Wagner in Bayreuth," that appeared in volume 7 (October, 1889, pp. 49-57) of *The English Illustrated Magazine*, a monthly edited by Macmillan from 1883 to 1893.[168]

The Wells connection was not quite so unsuccessful, but decidedly mixed. By the time Macmillan put out *Kipps* in 1905, Wells had already published *The Time Machine, The Island of Dr. Moreau,* and *The War of the Worlds* with Heinemann in 1895, 1896, and 1898, respectively; *When the Sleeper Awakes, Tales of Space and Time,* and *Love and Mr. Lewisham* (1899 and 1900) with Harpers; *The Sea Lady: A Tissue of Moonshine* with Methuen (1903); and *Twelve Stories and a Dream* and *The Food of the Gods* with Macmillan (1903 and 1904). Perhaps because *Kipps* was not vigorously promoted, it did not sell well. Between July 1906 and July 1907 only 180 copies had been sold.[169] Macmillan agreed therefore to let Wells out of his contract and approach another publisher. "I note your offer to relinquish my books," Wells wrote to Frederick Macmillan. "I like your firm in many ways. I don't think you advertise well and I think you're out of touch with the contemporary movement in literature. I don't think you have any idea of what could be done for me (but that you will of course attribute to the Vanity of Authors). But on the other hand you're solid & sound & sane."[170] In late 1907 Wells received an offer from Nelson and between the summer of 1908 and October of that year Nelson had sold 43,000 copies of *Kipps. The History of Mr. Polly* also went to Nelson in 1910. *In the Days of the Comet* and *Tono-Bungay* meantime had already been accepted by Macmillan and were put out in 1906 and 1909, respectively, but *Ann Veronica* was turned down, the plot being deemed, as Frederick Macmillan explained, "distasteful to the public which buys books published by our firm." Wells's latest novel went instead to Fisher Unwin. *The New Machiavelli* met with the same fate—though it was also rejected by other publishers until John Lane of The Bodley Head issued it in 1911. Macmillan did take up three other works by Wells—*The World Set Free: A Story of Mankind* (1914) and the novels *The Passionate Friends* (1913) and *The Wife of Sir Isaac Harman* (1914)—but he was by no means a Macmillan author in the way Matthew Arnold and Charles Kingsley had been at an earlier time and from 1914 until his death in 1946 Macmillan published nothing more by this startlingly prolific and successful writer. Publishing had, of course, become a much more capital-intensive business by the end of the nineteenth century and the relations of authors and publishers were much more determined by competition and commercial negotiations than had earlier been the case.

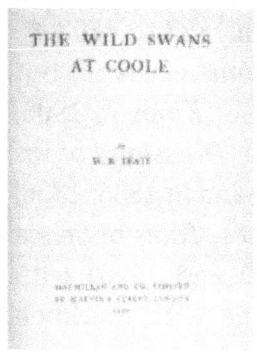

Macmillan also dropped the ball somewhat later in the cases of Max Beerbohm, Hilaire Belloc, Laurence Binyon, André Gide, and Herbert Read.[171] On the other hand, in the first decades of the twentieth century the company became the preferred publisher of some notable masters of English literature: 1923 Nobel-prizewinning poet W. B. Yeats (as of 1903); Indian poet and polymath Rabindranath Tagore, whose first collection of poems, *Gitanjali*, put out by Macmillan in 1913 won him the Nobel Prize for literature that same year; Sean O'Casey (as of 1925); and the prolific and immensely popular New Zealand born novelist Hugh Walpole (as of 1919).

*** *** ***

SOME LESS WELL-KNOWN SCOTTISH PUBLISHERS

Scotland was also home to a slew of minor printer-publishers, mostly active in the areas of theology, science and medicine, history, travel literature, reference works, and in one case, art books. Significant literary writings seem not to have emerged from these houses. Among them, the following were particularly active and enjoyed a considerable reputation.

A. & C. Black (Edinburgh) 1807

Founded in Edinburgh in 1807 by Adam Black (aged 23 at the time), the son of an Edinburgh master builder, the company—of which Black's nephew Charles became a partner in the late 1820s—moved to London in 1889 and was taken over by Bloomsbury Publishing in 2001. Adam Black had studied at Edinburgh High School and Edinburgh University before serving an apprenticeship with an Edinburgh bookseller, which he described as "a dreary, disgusting servitude, in which I wasted five of the best years of my life."[172] In addition to his activities as a publisher, Adam Black played a considerable role as a moderate liberal in Edinburgh politics, serving as Lord Provost (i.e., Lord Mayor) from 1843 to 1848 and as Member of Parliament for the city in 1856–65.

The firm is best known for putting out the third through ninth editions (1827–1903) of the *Encyclopaedia Britannica*, the brainchild of Andrew Bell and Colin Macfarquhar, who, with the help of editor William Smellie, published the first edition in Edinburgh in 1771. A. & C. Black acquired the rights to the *Britannica* in 1827. The Blacks also published a large series of travel guide books (especially to various parts of France), beginning in 1839; the annual *Who's Who*, beginning in 1849; other reference works, such as—under Adam Black's successors—*Black's Medical Dictionary*; some important new scholarly works, such as Frazer's *Totemism* (1887); and a number of practical "how-to" manuals. Having paid £27,000 for the copyrights and stocks of all Walter Scott's works, the company energetically promoted the production of Scott editions (and made a fortune from them). In 1902 it became the publisher of the immensely popular P. G. Wodehouse. Still, compared with Millar, Strahan, Foulis, or Bell & Bradfute, it was not a significant publisher of new works of literature. Its reputation rested on books of a more general character, science and medicine, theology, history, economics, sports, travel and guide books, schoolbooks, and books for young people.

Oliver and Boyd (Edinburgh) 1801

Thomas Oliver (1776–1853) and George Boyd (d. 1843) published many books and pamphlets in the first four or five decades of the nineteenth century on a wide range of topics: up-to-date medical research, ornithology, modern agriculture, travel and exploration, with volumes devoted to India, North America, Nubia and Abyssinia, Persia, Polynesia, and South America—the last in 1832 in the form of "a condensed narrative" in English translation, "with analyses of [the author's] more important investigations," of the celebrated *Relation historique du Voyage aux régions équinoxiales du Nouveau Continent 1799– 1804* [1805], *Vues des Cordillères et monuments des peuples indigènes de l'Amérique* [1810–13], and *Ansichten der Natur* [1808]) by the already eminent German explorer and naturalist Alexander von Humboldt.[173] History was another area cultivated by Oliver and Boyd—Scottish history above all, but not exclusively. A two-volume *History of Arabia Ancient and Modern* by the historian Andrew Crichton appeared in 1833, with a second edition the following year in the firm's "Edinburgh Cabinet Library"; a two-volume *Scandinavia Ancient and Modern*, also by Crichton, in 1838; a *Historical Account of British America* in 1839; and *The United States of America. Their History from the Earliest Period* in three volumes in 1844.

In literature, too, the emphasis was on Scottish works and writers—*Albyn's Anthology or A Select Collection of the Melodies and Local Poetry Peculiar to Scotland and the Isles, hitherto unpublished* (1816); Robert Burns (*Poems and Songs*, 1814); James Hogg (*Winter Evening Tales collected among the Cottagers of the South of Scotland* (1821); John Galt (*The Spaewife*, 1823); John Dunlop, poet, merchant, and sometime Lord Provost of Glasgow (*Oliver Cromwell, A Poem in Three Books*, 1829); Thomas Campbell (*The Poetical Works*, 1837). The firm also put out collections of "favourite songs" along with their musical scores (*The Scottish Minstrelsy*, 1814; the *English Minstrelsy*, 1815; *The Naval Syren, or The Cabin-Boy: Choice Sea Songs* (1815–36), guide books to Scotland, and some reprints, notably Goldsmith's *History of the Earth* (1830) and *History of Rome* (1843). In general, however, Oliver and Boyd seems to have been notably less active in promoting new literary writing than other companies founded by Scotsmen that have already been discussed. Some of those, it must be acknowledged, were from the start set up in London, and all ultimately opened branches in London or moved their publishing activities to the British capital. As Peter France and Seân Reynolds point out, by the 1850s, Edinburgh was no longer the dynamic literary and publishing center it had been in the first half of the century.[174]

James MacLehose (Glasgow) 1838

The son of a weaver in Govan, then an independent burgh, now a district in the South Side of Glasgow, James MacLehose opened a bookstore in Glasgow in 1838. He was a close friend of the Macmillan brothers, helped them in the early stages of their careers, continued to be consulted by them after they had established themselves as significant publishers in Cambridge and London, and occasionally co-published with them. Appointed bookseller to Glasgow University in 1864 and university printer and publisher in 1871, MacLehose chiefly published works on medicine, nursing, philosophy, mathematics, religion, and law, many of them by professors at the university. In addition, however, he brought out an occasional novel (e.g., *Effie Ogilvie, The Story of a Young Life* by the popular Scottish-born novelist Mrs. [Margaret] Oliphant, co-published with Macmillan, 1886), some translations (e.g., the satires of the French classical poet Boileau Despréaux), some classical texts, a few volumes of poetry, some in the Scots dialect, and an occasional play. Virtually all the MacLehose literary authors were Scots who have not entered the English-literature canon, although a few of the volumes of poetry, being reprints by MacLehose, must have enjoyed some popularity in Scotland and, to the present writer's surprise, have again been reprinted quite recently. Among the literary works put out by MacLehose, the following, in English, are worth noting: *Dan Daisy, or The Lady and the Sweep* (1850), a long poem with no author's name; William John Macquorn Rankine (Professor of Civil Engineering at Glasgow University), *Songs and Fables* (1874), including the witty poems "The Mathematician in Love" and "The Three Foot Rule" (https://mypoeticside.com/poets/william-john-macquorn-rankine-poems); John Nichol (professor of English at Glasgow University), *Hannibal: A Historical Drama* in iambic pentameters (co-published with Macmillan, 1873) and *The Death of Themistocles, a Dramatic Fragment, and other Poems* (likewise in iambic pentameters, co-published with Macmillan, and including among the poems a striking tribute to Abraham Lincoln, 1881); C. J. Ballingball Birrell, *The Two Queens: A Drama*, also in iambic pentameters (1889); William Freeland, *A Birth Song and other Poems* (1882); Archibald Hamilton Graham, *Poems* (1874); David Gray, *The Luggie and other Poems* (co-published with Macmillan, 1886; originally published by Macmillan in 1862); James Hedderwick, *The Villa by the Sea and other Poems* (1881); David Buchanan, *Man and the Years and other Poems* (1895; some in light Scots dialect). In Scots, the most notable volume was a collection of poems by the working-class woman poet Janet Hamilton, *Poems and Ballads* (1868), with a new posthumous edition, *Poems, Sketches and Essays* (1880).

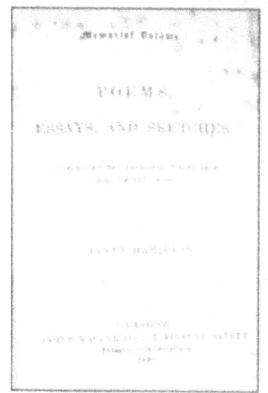

Gowans and Gray (Glasgow) 1846

This unusual firm was founded by Adam Gowans in 1846 as a printing and bookbinding business and continued by his son Charles Gowans in partnership with Adam's son-in-law James Gray. The firm ran into financial difficulties in the 1880s and, after the death of Charles, the partnership with Gray appears to have been dissolved, though the firm, which remained in the Gowans family, continued to operate as Gowans and Gray, located at 22 Ann Street and then 58 Cadogan Street in Glasgow. By 1908 a London branch had been opened at 3 Robert Street, Adelphi.[175] The impetus for moving the original firm into publishing and for its pursuit of a distinctive publishing agenda appears to have come from its later owner and director Adam Luke Gowans (1871–1958), a graduate of Glasgow University (MA, 1895) who was subsequently appointed (1944) head librarian of the world-renowned Glasgow School of Art, the first person from outside the School's ranks to occupy that position. Although we have been mostly, but not exclusively concerned hitherto with the eighteenth- and nineteenth-century contributions of Scottish publishers, Gowans and Gray made its impact in the early years of the twentieth century, the heyday of the "Glasgow Style" in the arts and the final phase of the city's boom time in general. Among Scottish publishers, it was unusual in its emphasis on the visual arts. However, it shared with firms like Blackie, Collins, and Nelson a policy of reaching out to a very wide market and thus, while keeping an eye on commercial advantage, contributing to the spread of culture among the middle and lower middle classes.

Under Adam Luke Gowans the firm was active in five main areas: inexpensive art books intended to be within reach of a broad upper working-class to middle-class public—the first Scottish publisher to win an international reputation in this area; contemporary Scottish poets and playwrights, together with some classics; translations of or books about foreign writers (French, German, and Spanish, but also Japanese); illustrated natural history books; and widely imitated—both in Britain and abroad—anthologies of poetry and short stories selected by Gowans himself.

Begun in 1904, the impressive series of "Gowan's Art Books," each devoted to a major European artist, from the Renaissance to the nineteenth century, and containing sixty black-and-white photographic reproductions of the works of the painter in question (by established photographers, such as the German painter and photographer Franz Hanfstaengl and the Frenchmen JacquesErnest Bulloz and Adolphe Giraudon) already encompassed fifty-two volumes by 1912, with more on the way.[176] They were sold at the incredibly low price of sixpence each with "pretty" parchment covers, one shilling for cloth-bound copies and two shillings for leather-bound copies. There was no text, only a few advertisements for other Gowans and Gray publications, for art magazines, such as *The Connoisseur*, and for the odd art dealer. A listing of booksellers abroad from whom volumes in the series could be purchased gives some idea of the potential range of sales. They include booksellers in France, Belgium, Germany, Holland (4), Italy (8), Portugal, Switzerland, Sweden, Canada, India, and the United States. Frequent reprints and new editions of virtually all the volumes testify to their popularity.[177] A companion five-volume series of "Drawings from the Old Masters," initiated in 1906 and produced along similar lines (sixty reproductions in each at a cost of sixpence for the parchment bound version), was devoted to works from the Albertina in Vienna; to Japanese prints in the British Museum, London, selected by the poet and scholar Laurence Binyon; to Dutch and Flemish drawings in the State Museum, Amsterdam; to "Famous Artists" in the British Museum; and to drawings by Claude Lorrain also in the British Museum and again selected by Laurence Binyon. The prolific German art historian Georg Gronau edited a volume of *Masterpieces of Sculpture from the Earliest times to the Present Day* (again at a cost of sixpence for the parchment bound version). Gowans also issued reproductions of individual art works, sometimes arranged in a series, as in the case of *Modern German Artists: One Hundred Masters of the Present Day* (1906). This was published in twenty parts, and as the reproductions were in color, the price was considerably higher—two shillings for each part or forty-two shillings for the complete set, bound in a single gilt-edged volume. According to Gowans's own advertisement in *The Connoisseur* for September 1905, *Modern German Artists* "contains what are, beyond all dispute, the best examples of colour reproduction yet issued."

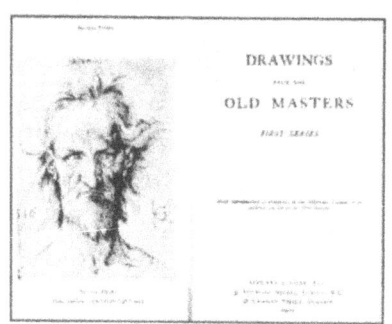

Gowans's enthusiastic love of the visual arts led him to employ the well-known and prolific Glasgow School artist, Jessie M. King, to illustrate many of his publications: notably *Our Trees and How to Know Them* (1908), one of twenty accessible "nature books" put out by Gowans and Gray[178]; Edmé Arcambeau's *The Book of Bridges*, about the bridges in Paris (1911); and *The Death of Tintagiles* (1909),[179] *Alladine and Palomides* (1911), and *The Intruder* (1913), plays and puppet plays by Maurice Maeterlinck in English translation in the series known as "Gowan's International Library." Over the three decades of their association Gowans also commissioned King to create books consisting entirely of her own drawings: *Budding Life: A Book of Flowers* (1908); *Dwellings of an Old World Town*, on the ancient, still perfectly preserved little town of Culross in Fife (1909); and *Kirkcudbright, A Royal Burgh* (1934). Among the major modern British writers published or republished by Gowans and Gray in the early years of the twentieth century we find *The Complete Works of Keats* in five volumes (1900–01) and, in the inexpensive sixpenny series entitled "Gowans's International Library," *The Haunted and the Haunters* (1906) and the play *The Lady of Lyons* (1907) by Bulwer-Lytton, *Goblin Market and Other Poems* by Christina Rossetti (1907, a reprint of the 1862 first edition), and *The King of the Golden River and other stories* by John Ruskin (1907); among French writers in the series: an English translation of the contemporary playwright Maeterlinck's *Interior* (1908), in addition to the three plays by the Belgian writer already mentioned, and Dumas Père's play *The Tower of Nesle* in an English translation by Adam Gowans himself (1906), *Le Cid* of Corneille (1908), *Les Chefs d'Oeuvre poétiques de Ronsard et de son École* (1907), containing "all the very best poems of the Pleïade," *Les Chefs d'Oeuvre lyriques d'André Chénier* (1907), and *Les Chefs d'Oeuvre lyriques d'Alfred de Musset* (1907), all in the original French, selected and edited by the contemporary French poet and critic Auguste Dorchain (1857–1930). German literature was represented by Theodor Storm's popular *Immensee,* already brought out by Gowans and Gray in a new translation in 1896, and by the same writer's tales *Eekenhof* and *Zur Chronik von Grieshuus* (both 1908), Arthur Schnitzler's puppet play of 1862 *Gallant Cassian (Der tapfere Cassian)* translated by Adam Gowans himself and published in 1914, and by E. T. A. Hoffmann's *Mademoiselle de Scudéry* (1908); Spanish literature by seven volumes out of a projected twelve-volume edition of the *Complete Works* of Cervantes (1901–03), by James Fitzmaurice Kelly's Taylorian lecture on *Lope de Vega and the Spanish Drama* (1902), and by Hugo Albert Rennert's *Life of Lope de Vega* (1904).

The range of Gowan and Gray's translations extended beyond Europe, however, above all—understandably in light of the current keen European interest in Japanese art—to Japan. The early 13th-century Japanese classic *Ho-jo-ki, Notes from a Ten Feet Hut*, advertised as "a famous Japanese classic," appeared with Gowans and Gray in 1907, as no. 15 of Gowans's International Library series and the same year saw the publication of *Japanese Fairy Tales told in English* by Basil Hall Chamberlain, as no. 13 of the series. A reissue of Frederick Victor Dickins's 1870 translation (the first) of the classic eighteenth-century puppet play *Chiushingura* by Takeda Izumo and others came out in 1910 (subtitled *A Japanese Romance* in Gowan and Gray's edition);[180] the following year saw the publication of *A Captive of Love*, "a quaint and charming *native* Japanese novel" in the words of the Preface, by the late eighteenth- to early nineteenth-century writer Kyokutei Bakin; this in turn was followed in 1912 by a translation by Frederic Dickins—just three years before the death of the pioneering Japanologist—of Rokuji-uyen's *The Story of a Hida Craftsman*, with Hokusai's illustrations in reduced facsimile. China was less well represented: *Chinese Fairy Tales told in English by Herbert A. Giles* appeared in 1911, as no. 38 of Gowans's International Library.

Probably the most influential of the Gowans and Gray publications, along with "Gowans's Art Books," were the firm's many anthologies of poetry and prose, classic and contemporary, mostly put together by Gowans himself and often presented as "The Hundred Best" in any genre. The following select list, arranged chronologically, will give some idea of the extent of this publishing program.

The Hundred Best Poems (Lyrical) in the English language, 1903 (37 editions down to 2010).

The Hundred Best English Poems, 1904 (seven editions between 1904 and 2007, featuring work by Arnold, Browning, Burns, Byron, Campbell, Coleridge, Cowper, Dryden, Goldsmith, Gray, Herbert, Herrick, Hood, Jonson, Keats, Lamb, Milton, Pope, Shakespeare, Shelley, Southey, Stevenson, Tennyson and Wordsworth, among others).

The Book of Love: One Hundred of the Best Love Poems in the English Language, 1905 (four editions between 1905 and 1914).

The Hundred Best Blank Verse Passages in the English Language, 1905 (11 editions between 1905 and 2012).

The Hundred Best Poems (Lyrical) in the Latin Language, 1905 and still being republished in 2018 (selected not by Gowans but by fellow-Scot and President of the British Academy, John William Mackail).

A Treasury of English Verse, 1906 (six editions between 1906 and 1928). This is a different selection from *The Hundred Best English Poets*, though with many of the same authors.

Poetry for Children. One Hundred of the Best Poems for the Young in the English Language, 1906 (seven editions between 1906 and 1918).

Lyric Masterpieces by Living Authors, 1908 (11 editions between 1908 and 1916).

Passages from the Hundred Best English Prose Writers, 1910 (held by 21 libraries worldwide)

A Second Hundred of the Best Poems (Lyrical) in the English Language, 1910 (eight editions between 1910 and 1920).

Famous Ghost Stories by English Authors, 1910 (nine editions between 1910 and 1920).

The Twelve Best Tales by English Writers, 1911.

The Twelve Best Short Stories in the English Language, 1912 (nine editions published between 1912 and 1930).

In a couple of prefaces, Adam Gowans explained what he hoped his carefully compiled anthologies would achieve. "It is the hope of the compiler," he wrote in the Preface to *A Treasury of English Verse*, "that this volume of poetry will become a favourite *House-book*, as the Germans call it, a book in which every member of the family will find some verses he loves, a book containing poems that will be read aloud by parents to children, by lover to lass, by friend to friend. It follows the course of life from its beginning to its end, showing its ups and downs as they have been reflected in the mirrors that great poets have held up to it. Nothing that is not good literature finds a place here; the book is intended to stimulate a taste for the best poetry in those who have never learned to love it and to revive it in those who have always loved it but have neglected it awhile." Similar sentiments are expressed in the Preface to *Lyric Masterpieces by Living Authors*, in which Gowans also deplores the copyright laws that make it difficult and, at the very least, expensive, for the publisher to connect readers of limited means with the leading literary figures of their own time: "So far as I know, no attempt has yet been made to publish an anthology confined to the verse of contemporary writers at so low a price [i.e., still the standard sixpence—L. G.]; I hope, therefore, that this book will attract many readers of poetry, whom the comparatively high price at which the works of most living poets are published has hitherto kept aloof. [...] I am of course sorry that I have been unable to obtain permission to include any of Mr. Swinburne's short lyrics, or of Professor A. E. Housman's." Still, a volume containing poems by Arthur Symons, Yeats, and Robert Bridges "must afford considerable compensation." Gowans goes on to contrast the situation in Britain, where "the expense of getting up even so small a book consisting entirely of copyright matter is a heavy one," with the situation in Germany, where "it is not the custom to make any charge for such permissions," thus allowing the publisher—Reclam, for example—"to publish for a shilling a volume of modern lyrics of 500 pages, in which no contemporary poet of any note is unrepresented," with the result that the German public is far more familiar with living German writers, such as Liliencron, Dehmel and Bierbaum, than the British public is with its contemporary writers.

In Gowans's aim of making good literature, including contemporary work, accessible to a broad public, and thereby enhancing the culture and quality of life of ordinary people, it is once again not difficult to discern the same project that, as we have repeatedly had occasion to observe, animated other Scottish publishers such as Blackie, Nelson, and Collins, and even Constable and Macmillan. Gowans's range was unusually wide, however, extending beyond English and even European literature and expanding the field to include the visual arts. In this respect Gowans probably reflects his time—the heyday of the then still dynamic international trading and industrial city of Glasgow in general and of the internationally admired "Glasgow style" in the arts and architecture in particular.

In addition, it should be noted that Gowans's popularizing project had considerable influence beyond Scotland and Britain. In France, the poet and critic Auguste Dorchain, who had edited volumes in French for Gowans and Gray, put out *Les cent meilleurs poèmes (lyriques) de la langue française* in 1905; in Italy, Luigi Ricci edited *Le Cento Migliori Poesie (Liriche) de la Lingua Italiana* in 1907; in Spain, Marcelino Menendez Pelayo, the director of the National Library, published *Las cien mejores poesías líricas de la lengua castellana* in 1908; in Portugal, Carolina Michaëlis de Vasconcelos prepared *As Cem Melhores Poesias (Líricas) da Lingua Portuguesa* for publication in Lisbon in 1910; in Germany Richard Moritz Meyer's edition of *Die Hundert besten Gedichte der deutschen Sprache (Lyrik)* appeared in 1909, followed in 1913 by *Die Hundert besten Gedichte der deutschen Sprache (Epik)* in 1913. In Holland, the Dutch poet and critic Albert Verwey brought out *De Honderd Beste Gedichten (Lyriek) in de Nederlandsche Taal*. The "Hundred Best" formula was carried still further in Spain in 1918 with the publication of *Las cien mejores poesías líricas de la lengua francesa, Las cien mejores poesías líricas de la lengua inglesa* and *Las cien mejores poesías líricas de la lengua portuguesa.*[181]

Gowans and Gray does not belong among the major Scottish publishing houses that we have described hitherto. It was smaller, but its distinctive character, directly reflective of the ideas and interests—especially in the visual arts—of its owner and chief editor, Adam Luke Gowans, would seem to warrant the relatively lengthy treatment it has been accorded here.

*** **** ***

With Adam Gowans we come to the end of our select list of Scots, often of modest origin, who founded enormously influential publishing houses, sometimes in the main urban centers of their homeland, Edinburgh and Glasgow, sometimes in the capital of the newly United Kingdom, in London itself. The number and influence of these publishing houses seems out of proportion to the relative wealth and population of eighteenth- and even nineteenth-century Scotland. Their existence, success, and contribution to the development and dissemination of English literature demonstrate the advantage, to both countries and peoples, of the Union that brought them together after centuries of rivalry and warfare—an advantage worth pondering in the current age of growing separatist and antiunion sentiment.

Notes

1. On the Nichols quoted here, see the entry in the *Encyclopaedia Britannica*:

   John Nichols (born Feb. 2, 1745, London, Eng.—died Nov. 26, 1826, London), writer, printer, and antiquary who, through numerous volumes of literary anecdotes, made an invaluable contribution to posterity's knowledge of the lives and works of 18th-century men of letters in England. Apprenticed in 1757 to William Bowyer the younger (known as "the learned printer"), who took him into partnership in 1766, Nichols undertook his first literary work as editor of the works of Jonathan Swift (1775–79). In 1778 Nichols became part manager of the *Gentleman's Magazine* and in 1792 sole managing editor. Of his original work, *Bibliotheca Topographica Britannica* (1780–90) and *The History and Antiquities of the County of Leicester* (1795–1815) are especially valuable. They are the fruit of his own meticulous observation and research. A friend of most of the leading literary figures of his age, he published Samuel Johnson's *Lives of the English Poets*, exercising much editorial influence and supplying a good deal of basic information. His own work as a biographer of the age began with his memoir of Bowyer, expanded into *Biographical and Literary Anecdotes of William Bowyer* (1782). This formed the basis of *Literary Anecdotes of the Eighteenth Century*, 9 vol. (1812–15; completed by his son, John Bowyer Nichols).

2. "Some of the greatest publishing firms in Britain today had their beginnings in Edinburgh and Glasgow . . . and a number of them still stand" (R. D. Macleod, *The Scottish Publishing Houses* [Glasgow: W. & R. Holmes, 1953], 7). "Firms were founded in Edinburgh, Glasgow, London, and Cambridge by Scots whose lists were to dominate the nineteenth-century literary marketplace" (David Finkelstein, *The House of Blackwood: Author–Publisher Relations in the Victorian Era* [University Park, PA: The Pennsylvania State University Press, 2002],

6). "The names of Scottish publishing houses would become firmly embedded in the cultural and social fabric of Britain and its colonies, providing printed material that informed and entertained, pioneering new techniques in graphics, illustration and production, and employing substantial numbers of skilled workers. [...] For a period at least Scottish imprints were among the most recognizable across the English speaking world" (David Finkelstein, "Publishing 1830–80," in *The Edinburgh History of the Book in Scotland*, vol. 2, Englightenment and Expansion 1707–1800, eds. Stephen W. Brown and Warren McDougall [Edinburgh: Edinburgh University Press, 2012], 96–106; here 106). Of "the great fixed stars in the publishing firmament," at the end of the nineteenth century, according to one historian, "Macmillan, Longmans, John Murray, Blackwoods, Smith Elder," who "had each a sort of magnetic or gravitational attraction and drew all the clients they needed into their respective orbits," four of the five were founded by Scots (J. Lewis May, *John Lane in the Nineties* [London: Bodley Head, 1936], 206–07). See also Frank Arthur Mumby and Ian Norrie, *Publishing and Bookselling*, 5th ed., revised (London: Jonathan Cape, 1974), 215 passim, and the excellent introductory chapter 2 in Patricia Thomas Srebrnik, *Alexander Strahan: Victorian Publisher* (Ann Arbor: University of Michigan Press, 1986).
3. John Gibson Lockhart, *Peter's Letters to his Kinsfolk*. 3 vols. (Edinburgh: Blackwood, 1819), 2:166–67, letter XLII.
4. The Londoners were also threatened by Irish publishers in Dublin. However, the Scottish and Irish cases were different. Books printed or published in Scotland were classified as "British" and therefore in principle duty free, whereas books printed and published in Ireland were "of foreign composure" and subject to import duties by weight. At the behest of the London booksellers and publishers, and also in some measure to protect themselves, the Scots clamped down on the steady and considerable flow of printed matter smuggled into small West Coast ports, such as Irvine and Saltcoats, from Dublin (Warren McDougall, "Smugglers, Reprinters and Hot Pursuers: The Irish–Scottish Book Trade and Copyright

Prosecution in the Late Eighteenth Century," in *The Stationers' Company and the Book Trade 1550–1990*, eds. Robin Meyers and Michael Harris [Winchester: St. Paul's Bibliographies, 1997], 155–59).

5. On the copyright issue, see Thomas F. Bonnell, *The Most Disreputable Trade. Publishing the Classics of English Poetry 1765–1810* (Oxford: Oxford University Press, 2008); Ronan Deazley, *On the Origin of the Right to Copy* (Oxford: Hart Publishing, 2004); John Feather, *Publishing, Piracy and Politics* (London: Mansell, 1994); John Feather, *A History of British Publishing* (London: Routledge, 2nd ed., 2006); David Finkelstein, *The House of Blackwood: Author–Publisher Relations in the Victorian Era* (as in note 2); Barbara Lauriat, "Copyright History in the Advocate's Arsenal," in *Research Handbook on the History of Copyright Law*, eds. Isabella Alexander and H. Tomás Gomez-Arostegui (Cheltenham, UK: Edward Elgar, 2016), 7–26; Lawrence Lessing, *Free Culture* (New York: Penguin Press, 2004), especially chapter 6; Alastair J. Mann, "'A Mongrel of Early Modern Copyright': Scotland in European Perspective," in *Privilege and Property: Essays on the History of Copyright*, eds. Ronan Deazley, Martin Kretschmer, and Lionel Bently (Cambridge: OpenBookPublishers, 2010), 51–66; Hector MacQueen, "Literary Property in Scotland in the eighteenth and nineteenth centuries," in *Research Handbook on the History of Copyright Law*, eds. Isabella Alexander and H. Tomás Gomez-Arostegui, 119–38; Warren McDougall, "The Emergence of the Modern Trade: Copyright and Scottishness," in *The Edinburgh History of the Book in Scotland* (as in note 2), 2: 23–39; Warren McDougall, "Smugglers, Reprinters and Hot Pursuers (as in note 4); David Murray, *Robert and Andrew Foulis and the Glasgow Press* (Glasgow: James MacLehose and Sons, 1913); Simon Nowell-Smith, *International Copyright Law and the Publisher in the Reign of Queen Victoria* (Oxford: Clarendon Press, 1968); Stephen Parks, ed., *The Literary Property Debate: Seven Tracts, 1747–1773* (New York: Garland Publishing, 1974); Trevor Ross, "Copyright and the Invention of Tradition," *Eighteenth Century Studies* 26, no. 1 (1992), 1–27; William St Clair, *The Reading Nation in the*

Romantic Period (Cambridge: Cambridge University Press, 2004); Kathryn Temple, *Scandal Nation: Law and Authorship in Britain (1750–1832)* (Ithaca: Cornell University Press, 2003). On Donaldson's contribution to eighteenth-century culture and enlightenment, see Yamada Shōji, *"Pirate" Publishing. The Battle over Perpetual Copyright in Eighteenth-Century Britain*, trans. Lynne E. Riggs (Kyoto: International Research Center for Japanese Studies, 2012).

6. On *Hinton v. Donaldson*, see Hector MacQueen, "Literary Property in Scotland in the eighteenth and nineteenth centuries" (as in note 5), 119-38.
7. Letter to Creech, May 20, 1776, cited in Bonnell, *The Most Disreputable Trade* (as in note 5), 37.
8. Letter to Creech, January 1, 1773, cited ibid., 35.
9. Bonnell, 53–54. Both Foulis brothers were interested in the copyright issue. In 1766 Andrew presented a paper on literary property at a meeting in Glasgow College of the Literary Society—which counted some well-to-do merchants among its members as well as professors at the College, and at which economic questions were discussed as well as literary and philosophical ones (*Some Letters of Robert Foulis*, ed. David Murray [Glasgow: MacLehose, 1917], 36–37)—and in 1770, at two meeting of the Society, Robert discussed "What would be the probable consequence of departing from the present law with regard to Literary Property and making that property perpetual?" (David Murray, *Robert and Andrew Foulis* [as in note 5], 49).
10. Barbara M. Benedict, "Readers, Writers, Reviewers, and the Professionalisation of Literature," *The Cambridge Companion to English Literature 1740–1830*, eds. Thomas Kaymer and Jon Mee (Cambridge: Cambridge University Press, 2004), 15–16; Ronan Deazley, *On the Origin of the Right to Copy* (as in note 5), 169–210; John Feather, *Publishing, Piracy and Politics* (London: Mansell, 1994), 64–96; John Feather, *A History of British Publishing*, 2nd ed. (London: Routledge, 2006), 55–56, 64–68; David Finkelstein, *The House of Blackwood: Author–Publisher Relations in the Victorian Era* (as in note 2), 6–7; Barbara Lauriat, "Copyright History in the Advocate's Arsenal,"

Research Handbook on the History of Copyright Law (as in note 5), 7–27; Kathryn Temple, *Scandal Nation: Law and Authorship in Britain (1750–1832)* (as in note 5), 116–20. See also the original documents in several important copyright cases in Stephen Parks, ed., *The Literary Property Debate: Seven Tracts, 1747–1773* (New York: Garland Publishing, 1974).

11. See the excellent outline of this aspect of earlier book publishing in William Zachs, *The First John Murray and the Late Eighteenth-Century London Book Trade* (Oxford: Oxford University Press for the British Academy, 1998), 28–35, 77–86. The complete "Checklist of Murray Publications" on pp. 255–409 of this outstanding work of scholarship gives hundreds of examples of publications in which John Murray I held shares, often along with fellow-Scot William Strahan and Thomas Cadell, the successor of fellow-Scot Andrew Millar. Some examples: a 1/64 share in Chambers' *Cyclopaedia* (1778–88), along with Cadell, Longman, Strahan, and thirty-two others; a 1/80 share in Samuel Johnson's *Dictionary* (1778) along with Cadell, Strahan, Longman, and twenty-one others; a 1/24 share in a third edition of Oliver Goldsmith's *History of England* (1779), along with Cadell and five others; a 3/100 share in the 60-volume edition, "with prefaces, biographical and critical" by Samuel Johnson, of *Works of the English Poets* (1779–80), along with Cadell, Longman, Strahan, and thirty-two others; a 1/12 share in a 10-volume edition of the *Works of Henry Fielding* (1784) along, once again, with Cadell, Longman, Strahan, and eleven others. In most cases, the main shares were held by the two, occasionally three, publishers whose names are listed on the title page. In *The English Novel 1770–1829: A Bibliographical Survey of Prose Fiction Published in the British Isles*, a comprehensive two-volume reference work edited by Peter Garside, James Raven, and Rainer Schöwerling (Oxford: Oxford University Press, 2000) one finds Constable often co-publishing novels with London publishers Longman or Hurst Robinson, Blackwood co-publishing with John Murray or T. Cadell. Sometimes the Edinburgh publisher is listed first, probably indicating that he is the primary partner, sometimes the London publisher is listed first.

12. Yamada Shōji, *"Pirate" Publishing. The Battle over Perpetual Copyright in Eighteenth-Century Britain* (as in note 5), 32.
13. See also MacQueen, "Literary Property in Scotland in the eighteenth and nineteenth centuries" (as in note 5), 128–29; Hugh Amory in *DNB*, vol. 38, 85.
14. Hall became a partner in the business early in 1748 when Franklin decided to devote his energies to other matters, a move not always appreciated by Hall, who complained to Strahan in a letter of December 1755 that the struggle with marauding Indians "employs Mr. Franklin so much that he has no Time to think any Thing about our particular Business, which gives me the more work." The partnership was dissolved in 1766, and David Hall took the printing and publishing business over on his own. Not without some acrimony, however: Hall reproached Franklin with lending support to a rival print shop and Franklin had to respond that, though he had indeed been offered an opportunity to become a partner in the rival business, he would refrain from doing so, as long as Hall provided him with more of what he, Franklin, felt he was owed. Strahan's influence thus extended to the New World. On Hall, see "David Hall and America," in J. A. Cochrane, *Dr. Johnson's Printer: The Life of William Strahan.* (Cambridge, MA: Harvard University Press, 1964), chapter 6, 60–91; also Leonard. W. Larabee et al., eds. *The Papers of Benjamin Franklin* (New Haven: Yale University Press, 1959–in progress), 37 vols. to date, with about 90 exchanges between Franklin and Hall from January 1748 until March 1772 and as many between Franklin and Strahan between 1743 and 1785; also the David Hall Papers, 1745–1822, at the American Philosophical Society in Philadelphia with letters between Strahan and Hall, Strahan and Franklin, and Hall and Franklin: Mss. B.H142.1-3 (https://search.amphilsoc.org/collections/view?docId=ead/Mss.B.H142.1-3-ead.xml;query=david%20hall;brand=default#detailedinventory).
15. Bonnell, *The Most Disreputable Trade* (as in note 5), 46.
16. David Murray, *Robert and Andrew Foulis and the Glasgow Press* (as in note 5), 26. Murray also quotes Gibbon as having observed: "As the eye is the organ of fancy, I read Homer

with more pleasure in the Glasgow edition. Through that fine medium, the poet's sense appears more beautiful and transparent" (ibid., 26). The Foulises' "magnificent folio edition" of the *Iliad* appeared in 1756, followed two years later by the *Odyssey*.

17. In Thomas F. Bonnell's words, the Foulises "idolized not the Elzeviers, but Robert Estienne or Stephanus, the Parisian printer renowned for his Greek lexicon, and Henry Estienne for his exquisite folio edition of Plato. The Foulis's bid for international acclaim was to be their own meticulous edition of Plato, a lavish folio of 'size and magnificence' for libraries. In the end, however, financial constraints led them to rely on smaller books for general use, books of 'elegance and neatness' delivering vernacular poetry. An Elzevier adapted to this end is what the age required; an Elzevier is what it got" (*The Most Disreputable Trade* [as in note 5], 40–41). On general appreciation of the "little Tully of Glasgow" (Warburton), i.e., the 1747 twenty-volume duodecimo edition of Cicero, see Murray, *Robert and Andrew Foulis and the Glasgow Press* (as in note 5), 23. In Murray's own view, this edition is "even yet the most convenient for the pocket."

18. Bonnell, *The Most Disreputable Trade* (as in note 5), 47.

19. Cited in Murray, *Robert and Andrew Foulis and the Glasgow Press* (as in note 5), 95.

20. "As printers and publishers, the Foulis brothers were famous for their magnificent editions of the classics, such as their splendid folio editions of the *Iliad* and *Odyssey* (1756–58). On the other hand, the great majority [*sic!*] of the Foulis brothers' book output consisted not of sumptuous showcase quartos and folios but of workmanlike octavos and duodecimo editions of classical and modern authors" (Andrew Hook and Richard B. Sher, eds., *The Glasgow Enlightenment* [East Linton: The Tuckwell Press, 1995], 13). See also on the Foulis brothers, Philip Gaskell, *A Bibliography of the Foulis Press* (Winchester: St. Paul's Bibliographies, 1986) and Richard B. Sher in T. M. Devine and Gordon Jackson, eds., *Glasgow*, vol. 1, *Beginning to 1830* (Manchester: Manchester University Press, 1995), 329–31.

21. Bonnell, *The Most Disreputable Trade* (as in note 5), 1, 51.
22. See Samuel Smiles, *A Publisher and His Friends: Memoir and Correspondence of John Murray*, condensed and edited by Thomas MacKay (London: J. Murray, 1911), 13.
23. Ibid., 22–26, 37, 75; George Paston, *At John Murray's. Records of a Literary Circle 1843–1892* (London: John Murray, 1932), 17–22.
24. Henry Curwen, *A History of Booksellers: The Old and the New* (1873; reprint Bristol: Thoemmes Press, 1996), 165.
25. On Murray and Austen, see Samuel Smiles, *A Publisher and His Friends* (as in note 22), 117–18. For a quick and attractive overview, see Margaret C. Sullivan, *Jane Austen Cover to Cover* (Philadelphia: Quirk Books, 2014), 11–19.
26. Richard D. Altick, *The English Common Reader* (1957; Columbus: Ohio State University Press, 1998), 263–64. According to Philip Gaskell, "as late as 1738–85, more than 90 per cent of the 514 books printed at Strahan's large London printing-house were in editions of less [*sic!*] than 2,000 copies" (*A New Introduction to Bibliography* [Oxford: Clarendon Press, 1979], 161).
27. On the publication of *Contarini Fleming*, see Smiles, *A Publisher and His Friends* (as in note 22), chapter 29, 315–21.
28. On *England and France: A Cure for the Ministerial Gallomania*, ibid., 228–31.
29. See Samuel Smiles, *A Publisher and His Friends: Memoirs and Correspondence of the late John Murray* (London: John Murray, 1891), vol. 1, 297–302, vol. 2, 245–46, 321–27, 349–55.
30. *Life, Letters, and Journals of George Ticknor* (Boston: Houghton Mifflin, 1909), vol. I, 58 (June 19, 1815); Samuel Smiles, *A Publisher and His Friends* (as in note 22), 114–15.
31. See James Raven, "The Novel Comes of Age," in *The English Novel 1770–1829: A Bibliographical Survey of Prose Fiction in the British Isles*, ed. Peter Garside (Oxford: Oxford University Press, 2000), 2 vols.; vol. 1, 15–121; and Peter Garside, "The English Novel in the Romantic Era," ibid., vol. 2, 15–103. A listing of the place of publication of new novels in Garside's article (p. 76) shows that the Scottish publishers based in Scotland significantly increased their role in the publication

of novels in the early decades of the nineteenth century: The numbers of novels published in Scotland rose from four, as compared with 714 in London and nine in Ireland, in the 1800s, to 29, as compared with 611 in London and four in Ireland in the 1810s, and to 100, as compared with 703 in London and 14 in Ireland in the 1820s.

32. See Samuel Smiles, *A Publisher and His Friends* (as in note 22), 41.
33. Cited in William Flavelle Monypenny and George Earl Buckle, *The Life of Benjamin Disraeli*, vol. 1 (London: J. Murray, 1910), 67. On the association of John Murray and Benjamin Disraeli, see Smiles, *A Publisher and His Friends* (as in note 22), 235, 255–57, 271–72; J. A. W. Gunn et al., eds., *Benjamin Disraeli: Letters 1815–1834* (Toronto: University of Toronto Press, 1982), 36–38; Stanley Weintraub, *Disraeli: A Biography* (New York: Truman Talley Books/Dutton, 1993), 54–65, 74–75; David Cesarini, *Disraeli. The Novel Politician* (New Haven: Yale University Press, 2016), 36–38.
34. For a list of books published by Robinson, see G. E. Bentley, Jr., "Copyright Documents in the George Robinson Archive: William Godwin and others, 1713–1830," *Studies in Bibliography* 35 (1982): 67–110.
35. On the Bell–Robinson challenge to Cadell–Strahan, see Richard B. Sher, *The Enlightenment and the Book: Scottish Authors and their Publishers* (Chicago: University of Chicago Press, 2006), 387–98.
36. A 15-page *Catalogue of Books printed for, and published by Bell & Bradfute, Parliament-Close, Edinburgh* (1795), includes the following (in octavo, except for Monboddo's *Ancient Metaphysics,* Reid's *Essays on the Intellectual Powers of Man* and *Essays on the Active powers of Man,* and Smellie's *Philosophy of Natural History,* which are in quarto, and Ferguson's *Institutes of Moral Philosophy,* which is in duodecimo):

- Adam Ferguson, *An Essay on the History of Civil Society. Sixth Edition.* 7s [s = shillings]
- Adam Ferguson, *Institutes of Moral Philosophy. Third Edition Enlarged.* 3s 6d [d = pence])

- David Hume, *Essays and Treatises on Several Subject. New Edition.* 2 vols. 14s
- Henry Home, Lord Kames, *Elements of Criticism. Seventh Edition.* 2 vols. 14s; *The Gentleman Farmer. Third Edition.* 7s; *Principles of Equity. Third Edition,* 2 vols. 12s; *Essays on the Principles of Morality and Natural Religion,* corrected *and* improved, 5s. Several other works by Kames are also listed.
- James Burnett, Lord Monboddo, *Of the Origin and Progress of Language. Second Edition, with large additions and corrections.* 6 vols. 2l (l = pounds sterling) 6s; *Ancient Metaphyics and the Science of Universals* 4 vols, 4l 4s
- John Playfair, *Elements of Geometry.* 7s
- Thomas Reid, *Essays on the Intellectual Powers of Man.* 1l 7s
- Thomas Reid, *Essays on the Active powers of Man.* 1l 1s
- Thomas Reid, *An Inquiry into the Human Mind, on the Principles of Common Sense, The Fourth Edition.* 7s
- William Smellie, *The Philosophy of Natural History.* 1l 1s
- Adam Smith, *The Theory of Moral Sentiments* [. . .], *to which is added a Dissertation on the Origin of Languages.* 2 vols., 14s.

37. On the limited market for books and their continued high cost until well into the nineteenth century, see Richard D. Altick, *The English Common Reader* (as in note 26), chapters 12 and 13 and *passim.*
38. On prices, see note 36. They appear somewhat lower than those cited by Richard Altick, *The English Common Reader* (as in note 26), 260.
39. Richard Altick, *The English Common Reader* (as in note 26), 268; Lockhart in his *Peter's Letters to his Kinsfolk* (Edinburgh: Blackwood [1819] 3 vols.), Letter XLII, vol. 2, 165–66.
40. A reprint of Constable's catalogue of books for sale at his store in 1800 is available from Amazon.com at https://www.amazon.com/Constables-Catalogue-Collection-Catalogues-Archibald/dp/1385461098?SubscriptionId=

AKIAI6MZ6I56PEDTRFEQ&tag=worldcat-20&linkCode=xm2&camp=2025&creative=165953&creativeASIN=1385461098

41. Publication ceased when Constable's company crashed in 1826, but was resumed six decades later under different ownership.
42. Raymond R. MacKenzie, "Archibald Constable and Company" in *The British Literary Book Trade 1700–1820,* eds. James K. Bracken and Joel Silver, The Dictionary of Literary Biography, vol. 154, Detroit: Gale Research, 1995 49–56; here 50.
43. Byron cited in Pottinger, *Heirs of the Enlightenment: Edinburgh Reviewers and Writers* (Edinburgh: Scottish Academic Press, 1992), 149.
44. Ibid.
45. Pottinger offers short, incisive sketches of each of the four founders: Smith (ibid., 56–60), Jeffrey (ibid., 60–66) Horner (ibid., 67–70), and Brougham (ibid., 70–76)
46. Cited in John Clive, "The Edinburgh Review," *History Today* 2, no. 12 (December 1, 1952): 844–50; here 847.
47. Pottinger, *Heirs of the Enlightenment* (as in note 43), 82–86.
48. On the numerous Edinburgh debating and discussion clubs, see the remarkable chapter IV, ibid., 42–55.
49. Ibid., 3.
50. Cited in John Clive, "The Edinburgh Review" (as in note 46), 845.
51. Cited ibid., 847 and Pottinger, *Heirs of the Enlightenment* (as in note 43), 3. Scott, whose work was then being published by Constable, was a generous contributor to the journal at the time, though he later defected and helped London publisher John Murray II to found the *ER*'s great rival, the *Quarterly Review.*
52. See Altick, *The English Common Reader* (as in note 26), 262–63.
53. On the Scott, Constable, and Ballantyne connection, Ballantyne's financial difficulties, Constable's helping out by purchasing the Ballantyne stock, and Ballantyne's ultimate bankruptcy, see Raymond R. MacKenzie, "Archibald Constable

and Company" (as in note 42), 52–53; R. D. Macleod, *The Scottish Publishing Houses* (as in note 1), 8–9; Thomas Constable, *Archibald Constable and his Literary Correspondents* (Edinburgh: Edmonston and Douglas, 1873), 3 vols., vol. 1, 138–39 (letter signed by Constable and dated May 31, 1809), and 382.

54. Anonymity was not unusual at this time, some authors preferring to define themselves by earlier publications, which thus received an indirect promotion: so, in Scott's case, "by the author of Waverley" or in that of John Galt, "by the author of *Annals of the Parish*."

55. See http://www.walterscott.lib.ed.ac.uk/biography/finance.html

56. Part 2 of the volume for 1814, put out by Constable in 1816, contains poems by Byron ("The Guerilla"), Wordsworth ("The Stranger"), Coleridge ("Isabelle"), Southey ("Peter of Barnet"), James Hogg ("Prayer of a Dying Soldier on the Field of Waterloo") and three unsigned sonnets. The bibliography of novels published in 1814 draws attention to many works by women novelists. In addition to Jane Austen: Mrs. Bridget Bluemantel (a.k.a. Maria Elizabeth Budden, 1780–1832), Laetitia Matilda Hawkins (1759–1835), Elizabeth Hervey (1748–1820), Barbara Hofland (1770–1844), Fanny Holcroft (1745–1809), Elizabeth Meeke (1761–1826), Sydney, Lady Morgan (1781–1859), Matilda Regina Roche (1764–1845), Elizabeth Isabella Spence (1768–1832), Ann of Swansea (a.k.a. Ann Julia Hatten, 1764–1838). For information about these and countless other women writers of this time, see the article of Peter Garside, "Mrs. Ross and Elizabeth B. Lester; New Attributions" (http://sites.cardiff.ac.uk/romtextv2/files/2013/02/cc02_n02.pdf); and the remarkable *Feminist Companion to Literature in English*, eds. Virginia Blair, Patricia Clements, and Isobel Grundy (London: Batsford, 1990).

57. Constable to Maria Edgeworth, August 19, 1823, and November 30, 1824; Maria Edgeworth to Constable, August 13, 1823, and January 19, 1825, in *Archibald Constable and his Literary Correspondents* (as in note 53), vol. 2, 405–12.

58. D. A. Low, "Publishing in the Eighteenth, Nineteenth and Mid-Twentieth Centuries," in *The New Companion to Scottish Culture*, ed. David Daiches (Edinburgh: Polygon, 1993), 256–59; here 258. See also Richard D. Altick, *The English Common Reader* (as in note 26), 287–89.
59. Correspondence reproduced in Thomas Constable, *Archibald Constable and his Literary Correspondents* (as in note 53), vol. 2, 491–99. According to Thomas Constable, the work in question, *The Life and Discoveries of Captain Cook*, which his father had declared to be "an indispensable article in his *Miscellany*, was never written" (ibid., 492).
60. The first volume of the *Miscellany* includes a four-page list (v–viii) of over fifty proposed future volumes. These include, besides many works of ancient and modern history and biography (including a "Life of General Washington" and the "Life of Benjamin Franklin by Himself," each occupying two volumes), studies of political economy and monetary systems, books on road making and railways, "Economic Cookery for the Rich and Poor," and "Devotional Exercises, Prayers, and Meditations." Constable's sense that inexpensive books would be instruments not only "for enlightening and entertaining mankind" but "for making money" (in the words of Scott's son-in-law and biographer Lockhart) is emphasized by Richard D. Altick, *The English Common Reader* (as in note 25), 207–08.
61. C. H. Timperley, *A Dictionary of Printers and Printing* (London: H. Johnson, 1839), 902.
62. See John H. Dempster, "Thomas Nelson and Sons in the late Nineteenth Century: A Study in Motivation," *Publishing History* 13 (1983): 41–87 (here 42), and 14 (1983), 45–63 (here 48n5).
63. On number-publications, see Richard D. Altick, *The English Common Reader* (as in note 26), 264–66.
64. See Alistair McCleery, "Thomas Nelson and Sons," in *British Literary Publishing Houses 1820–1880*, eds. Patricia D. Anderson and Thomas Rose, The Dictionary of Literary Biography,

vol. 106, Detroit: Gale Research, 1991, 218–24; Dempster (as in note 62), xiii, 43–44.

65. Sir Daniel Wilson, *William Nelson. A Memoir* (Printed for private circulation by T. Nelson and Sons, Edinburgh, 1889), 20–21.

66. Alistair McCleery, "Thomas Nelson and Sons" (as in note 64), 219. On the social, cultural, and political aspect of inexpensive series of literary texts, see John L. Kijinsky, "John Morley's 'English Men of Letters' Series and the Politics of Reading," *Victorian Studies* 34, no. 2 (1991): 205–25. Kijinsky cites the view that the great cultural project of the Victorian age, "its greatest task—and achievement lay in taming and 'civilizing' the dangerous engines of progress it had un-wittingly unleashed" in this case, mass literacy and mass distribution of printed material. Promoting the idea of an English national literature and culture, was, it is suggested, a way of moderating class consciousness and class conflict by emphasizing the people and the nation. J. R. Green's highly successful *Short History of the English People*, published by Macmillan in 1874, similarly "worked to establish for a wide readership a notion of a shared, organic English culture, one that united all citizens of the nation, regardless of class or region" (206–07).

67. Many of the Mühlbach titles, along with Hawthorne's *The House of the Seven Gables* (1851) and *The Scarlet Letter* (undated) may well have been acquired by Nelson's New York branch, as all those works appear to have been published first or at least simultaneously in the United States.

68. J. S. Bratton, *The Impact of Victorian Children's Fiction* (London: Croom Helm, 1981), 59, cited Dempster (as in note 62), 14 (1983), 5.

69. Returning to Scotland in 1847, Ballantyne learned that his father had succumbed to the heart ailment he had been suffering from for some time. A few years later, in the autumn of 1853, the death of his sister Madalina in childbirth led to a deep commitment to maintaining and spreading the

Christian faith. "From the time of the funeral, he started to attend church regularly [. . .] both morning and evening services. He formed a Bible-reading class for working men and was most assiduous in his duties, giving almost all his spare time to religious work of one sort or another. His newfound fervour so impressed the local clergy that, at the end of the following year [. . .] and at the age of only twenty-four, Bob was elected an elder of the Free Church of Scotland" [i.e., the evangelical wing of the church, led by Thomas Chalmers, that had broken away from the Church of Scotland at the General Assembly of 1843 in a move generally referred to as the Disruption—L. G.]. From this point in his life his letters become more heavily tinged with religious quotations and exhortations to godliness. [. . .] He abandoned a lighthearted book on which he had been engaged for his own amusement, and started to take an interest in the tortuous theological discussions and arguments in which the elders of the Free Kirk seemed to be constantly enmeshed" (Eric Quayle, *Ballantyne the Brave. A Victorian Writer and his Family* [London: Rupert Hart-Davis, 1967], 88).
70. The titles of those works indicate their emphasis on action and adventure: e.g., *Martin Rattler, or A Boy's Adventures in the Forests of Brazil* (1858), *The World of Ice: Adventures in the Polar Regions* (1860), *The Gorilla Hunters: A tale of the Wilds of Africa* (1861).
71. R. M. Ballantyne, *The Coral Island*, ed. J. S. Bratton (Oxford: Oxford University Press, 1990), Introduction, xvi.
72. Ruth Anne Thompson, review of J. S. Bratton, *The Impact of Victorian Children's Fiction* (New Jersey: Barnes and Noble, 1981) in *Children's Literature Association Quarterly* 9, no. 3 (1984): 134.
73. Cited in Dempster (as in note 62), 14, 20.
74. Between 1878 and 1881 educational titles represented 25 percent of Nelson's total output, but yielded 88 percent of the company's profit. Of that profit the Royal Readers alone represented some 45 percent. (Alistair McCleery, Introduc-

tion to *Thomas Nelson and Sons: Memories of an Edinburgh Publishing House*, eds. Heather Holmes and David Finkelstein (East Linton: Tuckwell Press, 2001), xviii.

75. Alistair McCleery, "Thomas Nelson and Sons" (as in note 66), 223.
76. See Valerie Joseph, "How Thomas Nelson and Sons' Royal Readers Textbooks Helped Instill the Standards of Whiteness into Colonized Black Caribbean Subjects and their Descendants," *Transforming Anthropology* 20, no. 2 (2012): 146–58.
77. On the remarkable success of Nelson as a French publisher, see the fascinating essay by Peter France and Siân Reynolds, "NELSON'S VICTORY: A Scottish Invasion of French Publishing, 1910–1914," *Book History* 3 (2000): 166–203.
78. In 1911 this Act was in turn repealed by Parliament, which extended the period of copyright validity to the life of the author plus fifty years. On the complex history of copyright in the Victorian era, see Nowell-Smith, *International Copyright Law* (as in note 5).
79. Kenneth Curry, *Sir Walter Scott's Annual Register* (Knoxville: University of Tennessee Press, 1977), 25–27; the praise for Coleridge was in a letter of May 16, 1812, to John Murray, 25. See also *Rocky Mountain Review of Language and Literature* 33 (spring, 1979): 85.
80. Cited in Alan Pratt's richly informative entry on "William Blackwood and Sons, Ltd." in *The British Literary Book Trade 1700–1820* (as in note 42), 17–25; here 18–19. Pratt's short work has been the chief source for the present section on Blackwood, along with Mrs. [Margaret] Oliphant and Mary Porter, *Annals of a Publishing House. William Blackwood and his Sons, their Magazine and Friends*, 3 vols. (New York: C. Scribner's Sons, 1897–98); F. D. Tredley, *The House of Blackwood 1804–1954* (Edinburgh: William Blackwood & Sons, 1954); David Finkelstein, *The House of Blackwood: Author–Publisher Relations in the Victorian Era* (as in note 2); and Robert Morrison and Daniel F. Roberts, eds., *Romanticism and Blackwood's Magazine* (Basingstoke: Palgrave Macmillan,

2013). On the "Cockney School of Poetry," the attacks on it by Lockhart and Maginn, and personal attacks in general, especially in the earlier years of Blackwood's, see the essays by Thomas Richardson (35–45), Tom Mole (89–99) and David Stewart (113–23).

81. See F. D. Tredley, *The House of Blackwood 1804–1954* (as in note 80), 90.

82. On their close personal and professional relationship, see the letters reproduced in Mrs. Oliphant, *Annals of a Publishing House. William Blackwood and his Sons, their Magazine and Friends* (as in note 80), vol. 3, 37–57, 65, 78–80 (on the *Romola* affair), 384–99. Of *Daniel Deronda,* Blackwood wrote Eliot in May 1875 that "re-reading many parts of the first volume ... has more than confirmed the admiration and delight with which I wrote and spoke to you after my first happy sitting over your MS. That first night I really felt like a glutton, dallying over his feast, and not reading at all with my usual rapid stride" (391). In March 1876 he wrote G. H. Lewes (to whom Eliot referred as her "husband"): "I read Book VI last night, and have unbounded congratulations to send to Mrs. Lewes. She is a *magician.* It is a poem, a drama, and a grand novel" (393).

83. See the statistical appendices in Finkelstein, *The House of Blackwood: Author–Publisher Relations in the Victorian Era* (as in note 2), 159–64.

84. *The Spanish Gypsy,* vol. XVIII of *The Writings of George Eliot* (Boston: Houghton Mifflin, 1908), Introduction, vi. Eliot's comment on John Blackwood is in a letter to George Henry Lewes's son, Charles Lee Lewis, October 27, 1879, in Gordon S. Haight, *The George Eliot Letters,* 7 vols. (New Haven: Yale University Press, 1854–55), vol. 7, 217.

85. On the Trollopes' visit and the trip to Skye, see Margaret Oliphant and Mary Porter, *Annals of a Publishing House. William Blackwood and his Sons, their Magazine and Friends* (as in note 80), vol. 3, 197–98. On the Blackwood–Trollope friendship in general, see 362–66.

86. Ibid., 363.
87. *The Life of Edward Bulwer, first Lord Lytton, by his grandson* (London: Macmillan, 1913), 2 vols., vol. 2, 467–68.
88. F. D. Tredley, *The House of Blackwood 1804–1954* (as in note 62), 153.
89. See Meldrum's letter to Blackwood, May 6, 1897, in Joseph Conrad, *Letters to William Blackwood and David S. Meldrum*, ed. William Blackburn (Durham, NC: Duke University Press, 1958), 3.
90. Cited in G. Jean-Aubry, *Joseph Conrad. Life and Letters*, 2 vols. (Garden City, NY: Doubleday Page, 1927), vol. 1, 206.
91. Frederick R. Karl and Laurence Davies, eds., *Collected Letters of Joseph Conrad* (Cambridge: Cambridge University Press, 1983), vol. 1, 367 and 409. See also Edward Garnett, ed., *Letters from Joseph Conrad 1895–1924* (Indianapolis: Bobbs-Merrill, 1928), 99 (Conrad to Garnett, July 18, 1897).
92. Joseph Conrad, *Letters to William Blackwood and David S. Meldrum* (as in note 89), 123.
93. Ibid., 173–74. Letter dated December 22, 1902.
94. See Joseph Conrad, *Letters to William Blackwood and David S. Meldrum* (as in note 89), 196–97.
95. F. D. Tredley, *The House of Blackwood 1804–1954* (as in note 80), 192. On William Blackwood's growing irritation with Conrad and the deterioration of their relationship, see also William Blackburn, "Conrad and William Blackwood," in Joseph Conrad, *Letters to William Blackwood and David S. Meldrum* (as in note 88), xxvii–xxxi.
96. Letter dated January 6, 1908, cited in G. Jean-Aubry, *Joseph Conrad. Life and Letters* (as in note 89), vol. 2, 65.
97. Letter to Meldrum, January 7, 1902, in Joseph Conrad, *Letters to William Blackwood and David S. Meldrum* (as in note 89), 138.
98. James Hogg, *The Brownie of Bodsbeck* (1818), *The Royal Jubilee* (1827); John Galt, *The Earthquake* (1820), *Annals of the Parish* (1822), *The Provost* (1822), *Sir Andrew Wylie, of that Ilk* (1822), *The Steamboat* (1822), *The Entail* (1823), *The Gathering of the West* (1823), *The Omen* (1825), and *The Last of the Lairds* (1826).

99. David Finkelstein, *The House of Blackwood: Author–Publisher Relations in the Victorian Era* (as in note 1), 119. On the declining role and influence of Blackwood's, ibid., 152–53.
100. Ibid., 94, 104–05.
101. Sidney Lee and George Smith, *George Smith. A Memoir with Some Pages of Autobiography* (London, 1902, "For private circulation" [Lee, 1–67; Smith, 69–143]), 71; see also [Dr. Leonard Huxley], *The House of Smith Elder* (London: Printed for Private Circulation, 1923), 1. (The author's name is mentioned only in an untitled opening note by "IMS," the widow of the last Murray Smith to direct the firm.) See also Lee and Smith, *George Smith. A Memoir*, 5–6, 25–26.
102. On the "Library of Romance," see [Huxley], *The House of Smith Elder* (as in note 101), 16–17, and Kathryn Chittick, *Dickens in the 1830s* (Cambridge: Cambridge University Press, 1990), 67.
103. Lee and Smith, *George Smith. A Memoir* (as in note 101), 26–27, 51.
104. Ibid., 88.
105. Ibid., 19–22 (Lee), 82–85 (Smith); also Thomas James Wise and John Alexander Symington, eds., *The Brontës, Their Lives, Friendships and Correspondence in Four Volumes* (Oxford: Shakespeare Head Press/Basil Blackwell, 1932), vol. 2, 139–256.
106. Lee and Smith (as in note 101), 103 (by Smith).
107. On Browning, see Arthur Waugh, *A Hundred Years of Publishing, Being the Story of Chapman & Hall, Ltd.* (London: Chapman & Hall, 1930), 78–79; on Thackeray, ibid., 70–73, 92; on Trollope, ibid., 89–95.
108. Lee and Smith (as in note 101), 113.
109. Cited by Barbara Quinn Schmidt in James K. Bracken and Joel Silver, eds., *The British Literary Book Trade 1700–1820*, The Dictionary of Literary Biography, vol. 154 (Detroit: Gale Research, 1995, 262). On the *Cornhill Magazine*, see the monograph of Spencer L. Eddy Jr., *The Founding of the Cornhill Magazine* (Muncie, IN: Ball State University, 1970. Ball State Monographs, no. 19).
110. Lee and Smith (as in note 101), 106–08 (by Smith).

111. Many stories and essays were in fact unsigned and that policy continued into the 1890s. As the historian of the company notes, anonymity was usual, except for eminent poets or deceased authors, such as the Brontës (*The House of Smith Elder* [as in note 101], 110–11). Even Trollope's serial in the early issues was anonymous, his name appearing only in the last installment (1864).
112. [Huxley], *The House of Smith Elder* (as in note 101), 110–11.
113. Arthur Waugh, *A Hundred Years of Publishing* (as in note 107), 92–93.
114. [Huxley], *The House of Smith Elder* (as in note 101), 99; Lee and Smith (as in note 101), 113.
115. Cited in [Huxley], *The House of Smith Elder* (as in note 101), 104. On Murray Smith's close relationships with Ruskin, Charlotte Brontë, Thackeray, and Mrs. Gaskell, ibid., 46–81, and Smith's "Reminiscences" in Lee and Smith (as in note 101), 119. On Smith's serving as pallbearer at Robert Browning's funeral and approaching the Dean of Westminster about having him buried in the Abbey, see [Huxley], *The House of Smith Elder*, 157.
116. Spencer L. Eddy Jr., *The Founding of the Cornhill Magazine* (as in note109), 2–3.
117. My source for much of this section on Collins is the excellent, eminently readable study of David Keir, *The House of Collins: The Story of a Scottish Family of Publishers from 1789 to the Present Day* (London: Collins, 1952). On William Collins's very early years, see especially 15–16, 20–24.
118. Ibid., 94–98.
119. Ibid., 32–33.
120. A reprint of volume 1 was published by Cambridge University Press in June 2013.
121. A list of books and pamphlets by Chalmers published by Chalmers and Collins follows a lengthy Appendix to *Speech delivered on the 24th of May before the General Assembly of the Church of Scotland* (Glasgow: Chalmers and Collins, 1822), and contains the following fourteen items, along with the price: *Sermons preached in the Tron Church*, 2nd ed., 10s. 6d.; *The Application of Christianity to the Commercial*

and Ordinary Affairs of Life, 4th ed., 8s.; *A Series of Discourses on the Christian Revelation viewed in connection with the Modern Astronomy*, 10th ed., 8s.; *The Evidence and Authority of the Christian Revelation*, 6th ed., 8s.; *The Importance of Civil Government in Society and the Duty of Christians in regard to it*, 3rd ed., 1s. 6d.; *Considerations on the System of Parochial Schools in Scotland and on the Advantages of Establishing them in Large Towns*, 1s.; *The Doctrine of Christian Charity Applied to the Case of Religious Differences*, 2s. 6d.; *Thoughts on Universal Peace*, 3rd ed. (originally published by Smith in 1816), 1s. 6d.; *The Utility of Missions ascertained by Experience*, 3rd ed. 1s. 6d.; *Sermon on the Death of Princess Charlotte*, 3rd ed., 1s. 6d.; *A Sermon preached before the Society for the Relief of the destitute Sick*, 2nd ed., 1s. 6d.; *An Address to the Inhabitants of the Parish of Kilmany*, 4th ed., 1s. 6d.; *The Influence of Bible Societies on the Temporal Necessities of the Poor*, 4th ed. 1s. 6d.; *Substance of a Speech delivered at the General Assembly in 1809*, 32nd ed. 1s. 6d.

122. On the breakup of Chalmers and Collins, see the detailed account, liberally quoted here, in David Keir, *The House of Collins* (as in note 117), 73-80.
123. Ibid., 217, 251.
124. Among them, Matthew Arnold, Jane Austen, George Borrow, Charlotte and Emily Brontë, Elizabeth Barrett and Robert Browning, John Bunyan, Robert Burns, Thomas Carlyle, Lewis Carroll, Samuel Taylor Coleridge, Wilkie Collins, Fennimore Cooper, Thomas De Quincey, Charles Dickens, Benjamin Disraeli, George Eliot, Ralph Waldo Emerson, Oliver Goldsmith, Nathaniel Hawthorne, Washington Irving, John Keats, Charles Kingsley, Charles Lamb, Henry Wadsworth Longfellow, Bulwer Lytton, Edgar Allan Poe, John Ruskin, Walter Scott, William Makepeace Thackeray, Robert Southey, Alfred Tennyson, Anthony Trollope, and William Wordsworth. Many of these authors were represented in multiple volumes. The series also included translations of a few foreign writers, such as Honoré de Balzac, Alphonse Daudet, Alexandre Dumas, Victor Hugo, and Jules Verne,

with Dumas and Hugo likewise represented by multiple volumes.

125. Agnes A. C. Blackie, *Blackie & Son 1809–1959* (Glasgow: Blackie & Son Limited, n.d. [1959]), 3. See also W. G. Blackie, Ph.D., LLD, *Sketch of the Origin and Progress of the Firm of Blackie & Son, Publishers, Glasgow, from its Foundation in 1809 to the demise of its founder in 1874* (Printed for private circulation, 1897), 8, 13–14. (Beautiful cover design by Talwin Morris.)
126. On the generally underestimated Glasgow publishing trade, which rose to about one third of total Scottish output in the mid-18th century until holding stable at around 25% or slightly higher through 1797, see *The Edinburgh History of the Book in Scotland*, vol. 2 (as in note 2), Introduction, 16–18. Edinburgh's advantage, "essentially derived from its monopoly on legal and official printing" (ibid., 15). During the copyright prosecutions, the Glasgow reprint publishers "openly reissued London publications." On the activities of the Glasgow printer Robert Urie, see Warren McDougall, "The Emergence of the Modern Trade," ibid., 29.
127. Agnes A. C. Blackie, *Blackie & Son 1809–1959* (as in note 125), 21.
128. See *Sketch of the Origin and Progress of the Firm of Blackie & Son* (as in note 125), 13–24.
129. Cited in Agnes A. C. Blackie, *Blackie & Son 1809–1959* (as in note 125), 8.
130. The later editions were available, still in two volumes, in duodecimo format for seventeen shillings, or in five still smaller 48 mo format for twelve shillings and sixpence.
131. On the roots of the goals and policies of major Scottish publishing houses in the national culture of Scotland, see the reflections of David Finkelstein, *The House of Blackwood* (as in note 2), 116–19.
132. The science and self-help books were published by the Gresham Publishing Company, a subsidiary set up by Blackie in London in 1898 to take on the subscription trade and to introduce scientific and technical publications. The Gresham Company also published the Imperial Edition of

Charles Dickens. On Talwin Morris's designs for Blackie, see the well-illustrated article of Gerald Cinamon, "Talwin Morris, Blackie and the Glasgow Style," *The Private Library* 3rd series, 10 no. 1 (spring, 1987): 3–47.

133. William Chambers, *Memoir of Robert Chambers, with autobiographical reminiscences of William Chambers*, 8th edition (Edinburgh: W. & R. Chambers, 1874), 54–59. The two Chambers' reading or "self-education," as William termed it, was, however, haphazard and undirected: "With Elder's field of literature laid open to us, Robert and I read at a great rate, going right through the catalogue of books without much regard to methodised study. In fact, we had to take what we could get and be thankful. Permitted to have only one volume at a time, we made up for short allowance by reading as quickly as possible, and, to save time, often read together from the same book. [. . .] Desultory as was this course of reading, it undoubtedly widened the sphere of our ideas; and it would be ungrateful not to acknowledge that some of my own success and not a few of the higher pleasures experienced in life are due to Elder's library in the little old burgh" (58–59).

134. Robert Chambers, *Traditions of Edinburgh*, new edition (1825; Edinburgh: W. & R. Chambers, 1868), Introductory Notice, ix–x.

135. *Memoir of Robert Chambers* (as in note 133), 152–55.

136. *Illustrations of the Author of Waverley, Being Notices and Anecdotes of Real Characters, Scenes, and Incidents Supposed to be Described in His Works* (Edinburgh: John Anderson, 1825), Preface, iii.

137. Cited in William Chambers, *Memoir of Robert Chambers, with autobiographical reminiscences of William Chambers*, 1st ed. (Edinburgh: W. & R. Chambers, 1872), 163.

138. Cited ibid., 227.

139. Ibid., 228. By comparison, "*Blackwood's Magazine* and the *Quarterly Review*, aiming at a more prosperous audience, averaged sales of less than 10,000 copies during the same period." (Lowell T. Frye, "W. and R. Chambers," *British Literary Publishing Houses, 1820–1880*, Dictionary of Literary

Biography, vol. 106 (Detroit: Gale Research, 1991, 83–91; here, 86).

140. William Chambers, *Memoir* (as in note 133), 237. The author of the letter, Allan Cunningham, was a Scottish poet and novelist and the author of *The Lives of the Most Eminent British Painters, Sculptors and Architects (1829–33)*.

141. Cited by Lowell T. Frye, "W. and R. Chambers" (as in note 139), 87.

142. Sue Thomas, *Indexes to Fiction in Chambers's Journal of Popular Literature, Science, and Art, later Chambers's Journal, 3rd to 6th series of Chambers's Edinburgh Journal, 1854–1910*, Victorian Fiction Research Guides, 7 (University of Queensland, 1989), 2.

143. Ibid., 1.

144. As an indication of Payn's former popularity, Princeton University Library holds over twenty of his novels, published after their serialized appearance in Chambers's *Journal* by Chatto and Windus in London or Harper & Brothers in New York, several volumes of short stories and essays, and a volume of his poems, along with his descriptive accounts of the Lake District. By 1883, fifteen years before his death, Harper had published 25 novels by Payn.

145. James Payn, *Literary Recollections*, 3rd ed. (London: Smith, Elder, 1884), 194. Payn, on his side, did not have a high opinion of William: "He was in no sense a man of letters; his style was bald, and his ideas mere platitudes; but because he had started the 'Journal' it was difficult for him to understand that its subsequent and permanent success was owing to his brother. Being childless and of great wealth, he was enabled to perform certain public acts [as elected Lord Provost of Edinburgh from 1865 to 1869, William Chambers oversaw the restoration of St. Giles' Cathedral, a program of slum clearance, and improvements to public health—L. G.], which cast Robert, who was weighted with a large family, comparatively into the shade. But there was really no comparison between them" (ibid., 141). Robert Chambers and James Payn, in contrast, were bound together by mutual affection and admiration. That William had a point, however,

in his reservations concerning Payn's work and editorial policy, is suggested by a modern scholar's judgment of a major novel by Payn, *Lost Sir Massingberd* (1864), to which a substantial increase in sales and circulation of the *Journal* was attributed: "*Lost Sir Massingberd* self-consciously and exuberantly plays its melodramatic, sensational and romantic elements to the hilt, indeed bordering on parody in its representations of the sickliness of Marmaduke Heath, the imperiled heir to the estate; the captive mad wife; and the romance between the sickly heir and the beautiful daughter of his rescuer" (Sue Thomas, *Indexes to Fiction in Chambers's Journal* [as in note 142], 3).

146. Cited by Lowell T. Frye, "W. and R. Chambers" (as in note 138), 87. Today's reader (2020) can hardly not be struck by the constant reference to the reader as a "man,"—not, it seems clear, in a generic sense but as a male. William Chambers does not appear to have thought that the creation of well-informed women was an important goal.

147. Cited ibid., 87–88.

148. See the vivid account of this period of Daniel Macmillan's life in the novelist Charles Morgan's lively, eminently readable *The House of Macmillan (1843–1943)* (London: Macmillan, 1943), 13–19.

149. For numerous examples, see *A Bibliographical Catalogue of Macmillan and Co.'s Publications from 1843 to 1889* (London: Macmillan, 1891).

150. Information on the Macmillans has been derived largely from five sources: Charles Morgan's *The House of Macmillan* (as in note 148); Rosemary T. Van Arsdel's essay in the Dictionary of Literary Biography, vol. 106 (as in note 63), 178–95; the same author's entry on the Macmillan family in the *Oxford Dictionary of National Biography*, 863–76; Elizabeth James, ed., *Macmillan: A Publishing Tradition* (Basingstoke, Hants.: Palgrave, 2002); and *A Bibliographical Catalogue of Macmillan and Co.'s Publications from 1843 to 1889* (as in note 149).

151. Letter dated May 22, 1856, cited in Morgan, *The House of Macmillan* (as in note 148), 28.

152. Letter from Hughes to Alexander Macmillan, September 25, 1856, cited at length in Morgan, ibid., 45.
153. Ibid., 57–58.
154. Cited ibid., 57.
155. On the Arnold–Macmillan connection, see Bill Bell, "From Parnassus to Grub Street: Matthew Arnold and the House of Macmillan," in *Macmillan: A Publishing Tradition* (as in note 150), 52–69.
156. Cited in Michael Millgate, "'And Sacred is the Latest Word.' Macmillan and Tennyson's 'final' text" in *Macmillan: A Publishing Tradition* (as in note 150), 131–52; here 132.
157. *A Bibliographical Catalogue of Macmillan and Co.'s Publications* (as in note 150), 80.
158. Cited in Andrew Murphy, *Shakespeare in Print: A History and Chronology of Shakespeare Publishing* (Cambridge: Cambridge University Press, 2003), 175.
159. The Virgil volume, for instance, published in 1871, was reprinted in 1873, 1874, 1877, 1879, 1880, 1882, 1883, 1885, and 1889; the Goldsmith volume, first published in 1869, had to be reprinted in 1871, 1874, 1878, 1881, 1884, and 1889 (*A Bibliographical Catalogue of Macmillan and Co.'s Publications* [as in note 150]).
160. John Morley, "On the Study of Literature," in *Literary Essays* (London: Arthur L. Humphreys, 1906), 335–84; here 341.
161. Sales were indeed impressive and most of the volumes in the series were frequently reprinted. J. C. Morison's Gibbon, for instance, published in May 1878, had to be reprinted in October of the same year and then again in 1879, 1880, and 1887; Leslie Stephen's Johnson, also published in May 1878, was reprinted in July of the same year and in 1879, 1880, 1882, 1885, 1886, and 1888.
162. Alexander Macmillan to Matthew Arnold, July 25, 1867, cited in Bill Bell, "From Parnassus to Grub Street: Matthew Arnold and the House of Macmillan" (as in note 155), 58.
163. Letter of March 18, 1902, to Frederick Macmillan, the eldest son of Daniel and for a time head of the New York branch. (Alexander had died early in 1896.) Cited in Morgan, *The House of Macmillan* (as in note 148), 154.

164. Reports cited in Morgan, *The House of Macmillan* (as in note 148), 119, 126.
165. It was 1901 before it was brought out by a major publishing company—Constable, as it happens.
166. Cited in Morgan, *The House of Macmillan* (as in note 148), 127–28.
167. Letters of January 22, 1885 (Macmillan to Shaw and Shaw to Macmillan), cited ibid., 128–29.
168. See https://babel.hathitrust.org/cgi/pt?id=mdp.39015056059655;view=1up;seq=66 (accessed July 5, 2018).
169. Charles Morgan, *The House of Macmillan* (as in 148), 146.
170. H. G. Wells to Frederick Macmillan, October 3, 1907, in *The Correspondence of H. G. Wells*, ed. David C. Smith (London: Pickering and Chatto, 1998), letter 698, vol. 2, 161.
171. Elizabeth James, "Introduction" to her edited volume *Macmillan: A Publishing Tradition* (as in note 150), 6.
172. A. Nicolson, ed., *Memoirs of Adam Black* (Edinburgh: Adam and Charles Black, 1885), 18.
173. *Travels and Researches in the Equinoctial Regions of America* (1832), edited and adapted by the prolific writer on geology, ornithology, and animals, William MacGillivray.
174. "By the 1850s, the heyday of Edinburgh as a literary center was over, and many publishers had either moved to London entirely or opened offices there. Nelson, too, had a London branch, but maintained its printworks in Edinburgh, where several large printing firms continued to flourish until the Great War" ("Nelson's Victory: A Scottish Invasion of French Publishing," *Book History*, 3 (2000) (as in note 77), 169.
175. *The Bookseller*, October 9, 1888, and January 24, 1908.
176. The first volumes were devoted to Rubens, Van Dyck, Rembrandt, and Raphael, but the series also included more recent painters such as Constable, Gainsborough, Greuze, Hogarth, and Ingres.
177. Thus, no. 1, on Rubens, published in 1904, had one reprinting in 1904, three in 1905, two in 1906, and two in 1907. A new edition, based on new plates, was issued in December 1907 and had to be reprinted in February 1908. The editor of a 1917 Cambridge University Press edition of

Hazlitt's *Selected Essays* recommended, in his introduction to the essay "On a Landscape of Nicolas Poussin" that the reader acquire volume 23 of Gowan's Art Books: "A little sixpenny volume containing sixty reproductions of Poussin's paintings can be obtained (Gowans and Gray publisher) and should be used by the reader in illustration of this essay" (219).

178. Twenty-one books were published in Gowans and Gray's series of "Nature Books": 1: *Wild Birds at Home*, 2: *Wild Flowers*, 3: *Wild Flowers* (second series; or part 2), 4: *Butterflies and Moths*, 5: *Wild Birds*, 6: *Freshwater Fishes*, 7: *Toadstools*, 8: *Our Trees and how to know them*, 9: *Wild Flowers* (3rd. series),10: *Life in the Antarctic*, 11: *Reptile Life*, 12: *Seashore life*, 13: *Birds at the Zoo*, 14: *Animals at the Zoo*, 15: *Some moths and butterflies and their Eggs*, 16: *Wild Flowers* (4th series), 17: *British Mammoths*, 18: *Pond and Stream Life*, 19: *Wild Birds* (3rd. series), 20: *Alpine Plants* (first series), 22: *Alpine Plants* (2nd. series). No. 21 in the series never appeared.

179. Gowans and Gray published an earlier edition of *The Death of Tintagles* in 1894.

180. On this classic work of Japanese literature in English translation, see Aaron M. Cohen, "The horizontal Chushingura," in *Revenge Drama in European Renaissance and Japanese Theatre*, ed. Kevin J. Wetman (New York: Palgrave Macmillan, 2008), 153–85.

181. See Patricia Anne Odber de Baubeta, *The Anthology in Portugal* (Bern: Peter Lang, 2007), 57–63.

Index

A. & C. Black, 100–01; *see also* Black, Adam
   Black's Medical Dictionary, 101
   Encyclopaedia Britannica, 1, 33, 66, 80, 100, 101
      William Smellie, editor, 1, 2, 23, 101
   publisher of P. G. Wodehouse, 101
   rightsholder of works of Walter Scott, 101
   travel guides, 101
   Who's Who, 101
A. Constable & Co., *see* Archibald Constable & Co.
A. and W. D. Brownlie, 73–74; *see also* Blackie and Son
   renamed "W. Sommerville, A. Fullarton, and J. Blackie & Co.," 74
Addison, Joseph, 14, 87
American War of Independence, 11
Anderson, John, 13,
   Anderson's Institution/University of Strathclyde, 13
Annual Register (aka *Edinburgh Annual Register*), 33, 46, 47, 48; *see also* Archibald Constable & Co.
   Edmund Burke, editor, 47
Archibald Constable & Co., 1, 14, 19, 26–38; *see also* Constable, Archibald
   Constable's Miscellany series, 34, 35, 36, 37, 82
   early novels published, 30–31
   Edinburgh Annual Register (aka *Annual Register*), 33, 47
      and Walter Scott, 33
   Edinburgh Review, 27, 28, 30, 32
      and John Ballantyne & Co., 48
   The Scots Magazine and Edinburgh Literary Miscellany, 27; 50 51
   titles published, 37–38
Arnold, Matthew, 14, 63, 65, 80, 92, 93, 96, 100; *see also* Macmillan
   Anarchy and Authority, later *Culture and Anarchy*, 65
   Essays in Criticism, 95
   New Poems, 95
Austen, Jane; *see also* Bell & Bradfute, John Murray, Thomas Nelson
   Emma, 17
   Mansfield Park, 17, 24
   Northanger Abbey (originally *Susan*), 17, 24
   Pride and Prejudice (originally *First Impressions*), 17, 24
   Sense and Sensibility (originally *Elinor and Marianne*), 17, 24

Bacon, Francis, 3, 77, 87, 93
Bage, Robert, 49
   Barham Downs, 49
   James Wallace, 49
   Mount Henneth, 49
Baillie, Joanna, 31, 47, 60, 76
Ballantyne, James, 42
   James Ballantyne & Co., 32, 33, 49

Ballantyne, James (*cont.*)
  printer of Sir Walter Scott, 19, 42, 46
Ballantyne, John, 46; *see also* John Ballantyne & Co.
Ballantyne, R. M.
  clerk of the Hudson's Bay Company, 42
  early author of children's books, 42
  The Coral Island: A Tale of the Pacific Ocean, 42
  Hudson's Bay, or Everyday Life in the Wilds of North America, 42
  The Northern Coasts of America and the Hudson's Bay Territories: A Narrative of Discovery and Adventure, 42
  Snowflakes and Sunbeams, or, The Young Fur Traders, 41
  Ungava: A Tale of Esquimaux Land, 42
Barrow, Sir John
  Life of Peter the Great, 20
Beccaria, Cesare
  Discourse on Public Oeconomy and Commerce, 16
Becket, Thomas, 4, 10
  apprentice of Andrew Millar, 10
  publisher, 10, 23
Bell, Andrew, 1, 101
  engraver, 1
Bell, Catherine D.
  The Children's Mirror, or What is my Likeness?, 43
  Kind Words to Domestic Servants, 43
  Love Thy Neighbour as Thyself, or The Story of Mike, the Irish Boy, 43
  Mind Your Own Business, 43
  The Way to be Happy, or The Story of Willie, the Gardener Boy, 43
Bell, Currer, pseudonym of Charlotte Brontë, 61

Bell, John, 22–26; *see also* Bell & Bradfute
  apprentice to Alexander Kincaid, 22
  pirated editions, 22–23
    Essay on the History of Civil Society (Adam Ferguson), 25
    A Father's Legacy to his Daughters (John Gregory), 23
    Letters to his Son (Lord Chesterfield), 23
    A Sentimental Journey (Laurence Sterne), 23
    Works (Laurence Sterne), 23
  rights to Thomas Reid's *Essays on the Intellectual Powers of Man*, 23
Bell & Bradfute, 22–26
  book prices, 25–26
  collaboration with other publishers, 23–24
  literary publisher, 23–25
  onetime publisher of Jane Austen, 24
  "pirated editions," 23
Belloc, Hilaire, 100
  On Anything, 38
Besant, Walter
  The Ivory Gate, 85
  The Master Craftsman, 85
Binyon, Lawrence, 99, 106
  Paris and Oenone, 37
Birch, Rev. Thomas
  translator of Pierre Bayle's *Dictionary*, 8
Birrell, C. J. Ballingball, 104
  The Two Queens: A Drama, 104
Black, Adam, 100, 101; *see also* A. & C. Black
  Lord Provost of Edinburgh, 100
Black, Charles, 100
Blackie, Agnes A. C., 73

Blackie, John, 73
  bookseller, 73–74
  early life, 73
Blackie, John Jr., 74, 76
Blackie, Robert, 75
Blackie, Walter, 78
  Hill House, 78
Blackie, William Graham, 75
Blackie & Son, 73–79
  and A. and W. D. Brownlie, 74
  Blackie & Sons, Ltd. [printer/publisher], 75
    historiography, 75
      Ranke's *Popes of Rome*, 75
    reference works, 75
      The Imperial Bible Dictionary, 75
      The Imperial Family Bible, 75
    reward books, 77—78
      famous authors, 77
    technical publisher, 75
      The Engineer and Machinist's Assistant, 75
      The Engineer and Machinist's Drawing Book, 75
      The Horse: Its Treatment in Health and Disease, 79
      Machinery and Mill Work, 75
      The Modern Baker, Confectioner and Caterer, 79
      The Modern Carpenter and Joiner, 79
      Modern House Construction, 79
      Modern Power Generators, 79
      Railway Machinery, 75
      Steam Engines: A Treatise on Steam Engines and Boilers, 75
  Blackie's English Classics, 77
    famous contributors, 77
  Blackie Red Letter series, 78
  Casquet of Literary Gems, 76
    famous Scottish contributors, 76
  international branches, 78
  reissued series, 77
    famous contributors, 77
  Talwin Morris as art director, 79–80
    Glasgow School, 78
  "W. G. Blackie & Co." [printer], 75
Blackwood, John
  "little Editor," 52
  publisher of George Eliot, 52
Blackwood, William, 7, 50
  antiquarian bookseller, 50
  apprentice at Bell & Bradfute, 50
  as publisher, 50–52
    Edinburgh Monthly Magazine/Blackwood's Edinburgh Magazine, 50–53
Blackwood, William III, 55
  as publisher of Joseph Conrad, 55–57
Blair, Hugh
  Essays on Rhetoric, 16
Blake, William, 16, 77, 93
Boileau-Despréaux, Nicolas de, 14, 103
booksellers, 3–5, 7, 8, 9, 28, 39, 58, 74, 80, 106
Borrow, George, 77
  The Bible in Spain, 31
  Lavengro, 31
  Romany Rye, 31
  Tales of the Wild and the Wonderful, 31
Bossuet, Jacques-Bénigne, 14
Boyd, George, 101
Bradfute, John, 23, 24
  nephew and apprentice of John Bell, 23
Brewster, Sir David
  Life of Sir Isaac Newton, 20
Brontë, Charlotte, 45, 60, 61, 66, 73, 84; *see also* Smith, George Murray

Brontë, Charlotte (*cont.*)
  as Currer Bell, 61
  Emma, 17
  friendship with George Murray
    Smith, 19, 61, 64
  Jane Eyre, 61
  Life of Charlotte Brontë by Mrs.
    Gaskell, 61
  Poems by Currer, Ellis, and Acton Bell,
    61
  portrait by George Richmond, 61
  The Professor, 60, 61
  Shirley, 61
  Villette, 61
  "Watching and Wishing," 63
Brontë, Emily, 63
  "The Outcast Mother," 63
Browning, Elizabeth Barrett, 80
  The Cry of the Children, 52
  "A Forced Recruit at Solferino," 63
  "A Musical Instrument," 63
  and George Murray Smith, 64
Browning, Robert, 12, 62, 64
  and George Murray Smith, 61, 62,
    64, 65
  The Ring and the Book, 61–62
Brunton, Mary
  Emmeline, 31
Buchan, John, 44
  John Burnett of Barns: A Romance, 85
  The Thirty-Nine Steps, 57
Buchanan, David
  Man and the Years and other Poems,
    104
Buchanan, George
  English version of *Rerum Scoticarum*
    Historia, 74
Bulwer-Lytton, Edward, 24, 45, 54, 77,
    107; *see also* William
    Blackwood and Sons

The Coming Race, 54
Eugene Aram, 24
Kenelm Chillingly, His Adventures and
  Opinions, 54
The Last Days of Pompeii, 24
The Parisians, 54
Bunyan, John, 45, 71, 78, 93
  Pilgrim's Progress, 74
Burnett, James, Lord Monboddo
  Of the Origin and Progress of
    Language, 26
Burney, Fanny, 9
Burns, Robert, 9, 45, 72, 81, 87, 94,
    109
  Poems and Songs, 102
  The Works of Robert Burns, 39
Byron, George Gordon, Lord, 17, 27,
    28, 29, 48, 71, 72, 76, 77,
    109
  Childe Harold's Pilgrimage, 50
  Complete Works, 17, 18
  "The Corsair," 17
  friendship with Walter Scott, 19
  "The Guerilla," 33
  Ode to Napolean Bonaparte, 17
  statue of, 18

Cadell, Thomas, 4, 7; *see also* Millar,
    Andrew
  examples of famous titles
    published, 9
  onetime apprentice of Andrew
    Millar, 9
Campbell, Thomas, 28, 48, 76, 102,
    109
  The Poetical Works, 102
Carlyle, Thomas, 45
Carroll, Lewis, 78, 95; *see also*
    Macmillan

INDEX

Alice's Adventures in Wonderland, 95
Hunting of the Snark, 95
Sylvie and Bruno, 95
Through the Looking Glass, 95
Cervantes, Miguel de, 14, 45, 77, 108
   Don Quixote, 8, 49, 80
Chalmers, Charles, 69, 70; see also
   Chalmers and Collins,
   William Collins
   partnership with Collins, 69–70
Chalmers, Thomas, 28, 60, 67–70
   evangelist, 67, 68, 69
   friendship with William Collins, 67, 70
   Application of Christianity to the Commercial and Ordinary Affairs of Life, 69
   Astronomical Discourses, 68
   The Christian and Civic Economy of Large Towns, 69
   The Collected Works of Thomas Chalmers, 71
   The Importance of Civil Government to Society and the Duty of Christians in regard to it, 69
   Political Economy in Connection with the Moral State and Moral Prospects of Society, 71
   Scripture References, designed for the use of Parents, Teachers and private Christians, 69
   A Series of Discourses on the Christian Revelation, 69
   On the Sufficiency of the Parochial System, without a Poor Rate, for the Right Management of the Poor, 71
   The Supreme Importance of a Right Moral to a Right Economic State of the Community, 71
   Tracts of Pauperism, 71
Chalmers and Collins, 69–70; see also
   Chalmers, Charles; Collins, William
   financial difficulties of, 70
Chamberlain, Basil Hall
   Japanese Fairy Tales told in English, 108
Chambers, Robert, 79, 81, 82; see also
   W. & R. Chambers
   bookstall, 80–81
   calligrapher, 80
   Cyclopaedia of English Literature: A History, Critical and Biographical, of British Authors, in All Departments of Literature, Illustrated by Specimens of Their Writings, 87
   De Officiis (An Essay on Moral Duty), 25
   friendship with Sir Walter Scott, 82
   History of the Rebellions in Scotland in 1745–1746, 36
   History of the Rebellions in Scotland, under Montrose and Others, from 1638 till 1660, 37
   History of the Rebellions in Scotland under the Viscount of Dundee and the Earl of Mar in 1689 and 1715 Cicero, 37
   Illustrations of the Author of Waverley, 81
   literary editor of Chambers' Edinburgh Journal, 82
   Orationes selectae, 25
   Popular Rhymes of Scotland, 82
   Traditions of Edinburgh, 82
Chambers, William, 79; see also W. & R. Chambers
   bookseller's apprentice, 80

Chambers, William (*cont.*)
   managing editor of *Chambers'
      Edinburgh Journal,* 82
   Memoir of Robert Chambers, 80, 84
Chateaubriand, François-René de, 46,
      79
   The Last of the Abencerages, 25
Clare, John, "peasant poet," 59, 76
Coleridge, Samuel, 72, 76, 77, 93, 109
   Christabel, 19
   "Isabelle," 33
Collins, Wilkie, 64, 65, 66
   Armadale, 65
Collins, William, 66
   early years, 66–67
   Temperance Society founder, 67
   and Thomas Chalmers, 67–69
Collins, William II, 71–73
   educational publications, 71
   Lord Provost of Glasgow, 71
   Popular Poets series, 71–72
Collins, William III, 72
   Collins Illustrated Pocket Classics,
      72
      canonical writers included in
         series, 72–73
   international expansion of William
      Collins, 72
Colquhoun, John Campbell
   Zoe: An Athenian Tale, 31
Congreve, William, 14, 77
Conrad, Joseph, 44, 54–57; *see also*
      William Blackwood and Sons
   Almayer's Folly, 54
   The End of the Tether, 56
   The Heart of Darkness, 55
   "The Idiots," 54
   Karain: A Memory, 55
   "The Lagoon," 54, 65
   Lord Jim, 56
   The Nigger of 'The Narcissus,' 55

   An Outcast of the Islands, 54
   The Rescue, 55
   "A Victim of Progress" later "An
      Outpost of Progress," 54
   "The Youth," 55
Constable, Archibald, 2, 7, 19; *see also*
      Archibald Constable & Co.
Constable, Thomas, 37
   antiquarian bookseller, 26
   printer to Edinburgh University, 37
   printer to Queen Victoria, 37
Constable's Miscellany, 34–37
   early texts, 36
   financing of, 35–36
   works of Robert Chambers in,
      History of the Rebellion of 1745, 82
      *History of the Rebellions in Scotland
         in 1689 and 1715,* 82
Cooper, James Fenimore, 12, 79
Copyright Act, 46
copyright law, 3–6, 9, 21, 22, 110
Cornelius Nepos, 14
   Vitae excellentium imperatorum, 25
The Cornhill, 62–65; *see also* Smith,
      Elder, and Co.; Smith,
      George Murray
   dinners and regular guests, 63–64
Cowper, William, 72, 76, 93, 109
   Poems, 39
Crabbe, George, 18, 19, 29, 87
Creech, William, 4, 9, 22
Crichton, Andrew
   Historical Account of British America,
      102
   History of Arabia Ancient and Modern,
      102
   Scandinavia Ancient and Modern, 102
   *The United States of America. Their
      History from the Earliest Period,*
      102
Crosby, Benjamin, 17

INDEX

Crumpe, M. G. T.
   Isabel St. Albe, or Vice and Virtue. A Novel, 31
Cumberland, Richard
   Henry, 49
Cuthbertson, Catherine
   The Hut and the Castle, 31

Dalyell, Sir John Graham
   Fragments of Scottish History, 26
Darwin, Charles, 45, 64
   Origin of Species, 21
De la Mare, Walter, 73
   A Child's Day, 38
   The Listeners and other poems, 38
   Peacock Pie, 38
Defoe, Daniel, 19, 73, 77, 79, 87, 93, 94
   Robinson Crusoe, 39
De Quincey, Thomas, 77, 84
   The English Mail-Coach, 52
   On Murder Considered as One of the Fine Arts, 52
Dick, Thomas
   The Christian Philosopher, 69
Dickens, Charles, 41, 44, 45, 73, 78
Disraeli, Benjamin, 20, 45
   Contarini Fleming. A Psychological Auto-Biography, 18
   England and France, or A Cure for the Ministerial Gallomania, 18
D'Israeli, Isaac, 15, 18, 20, 76
   Curiosities of Literature, 15
   Despotism, or The Fall of the Jesuits: A Political Romance, 18
   Flim-Flams, or The Life and Errors of my Uncle and the Amours of my Aunt, 18
   Romances, 18
   Vaurien, 18
Donaldson, Alexander, 4, 22
Donaldson v. Beckett, 9
Dorchain, Auguste, 107, 111
Doyle, Arthur Conan
   "The Mystery of Sasassa Valley," 85
   The White Company, 65
Dryden, John, 14, 71, 76, 109
Dumas, Alexandre, père, 45, 79, 95
   The Black Tulip, 41
   The Queen's Necklace, 41
   The Tower of Nesle, 107
Dunbar, William, 14, 76
Dunlop, John, 102
   Oliver Cromwell, A Poem in Three Books, 102

Eastlake, Charles
   translator of Goethe's *Theory of Colours*, 21
Edgeworth, Maria, 29, 34, 85
   Helen, 24
Edinburgh Annual Register, 33, 46–47
   takeover by Archibald Constable & Co., 33
Edinburgh debating clubs
   Academy of Physicks, 29
   Friday Club, 29
   Poker Club, 29
Edinburgh Review, 7, 19, 27, 29 46
   examples of famous authors reviewed, 29
   famous contributors, 28
      Campbell, Thomas, 28, 48, 76, 109
      Carlyle, Thomas, 18, 28, 45, 77, 94
      Chalmers, Thomas, 28
      Hazlitt, William, 28
      Macaulay, Thomas Babbington, 28
      Mackintosh, Sir James, 28
         Vindiciae Gallicae, 28

Edinburgh Review (*cont.*)
   Malthus, T. R., 28
   Moore, Thomas, 28
   Palgrave, Francis, 28
   Playfair, John, 28
   Scott, Sir Walter, 28
  founders, 27
   Brougham, Henry, 27, 29, 30
   Horner, Francis, 27
   Jeffrey, Francis, 27, 28, 29
   Smith, Reverend Sydney, 27
  payment to contributors, 27, 28
education
  emphasis of in Scotland, 1, 35, 77–78
Education Acts of 1870 and 1872, 44, 77
1842 Copyright Act, 46
Eliot, George, 41, 52, 53, 63, 65, 73; *see also* William Blackwood and Sons
  Adam Bede, 52
  Daniel Deronda, 53
  Felix Holt the Radical, 53
  Middlemarch, 53
  The Mill on the Floss, 52
  Romola, 53
    fee paid for, 65
  Scenes of Clerical Life, 52
  Silas Marner, 53
  The Spanish Gypsy, 53
  Works, 53
Ellis, Havelock
  The Dance of Life, 38
  Impressions and Comments, 38
Elzevir, *see* Estienne, Robert (aka Robertus Stephanus)
Encyclopaedia Britannica, 1, 33, 66, 80, 101

Erskine, John, 26
  Doctrinal and Occasional Sermons, 26
Estienne, Robert (aka Robertus Stephanus), 13, 15

Fénelon, François, 14
  Les Aventures de Télémaque, 25
Ferguson, Adam, 12, 29, 23
  Essay on the History of Civil Society, 25
  Institutes of Moral Philosophy, 25
Ferguson, Robert
  editor of *The Natural History of Insects*, 20
Fielding, Henry, 4, 24
  Amelia, 8, 49
  Jonathan Wild, 8, 49
  Joseph Andrews, 8, 49
  "The Novels of Henry Fielding, Esq.," 49
  Tom Jones, 8, 24, 49
  Works of Henry Fielding, 8, 16
Forster, E. M., 58
  Howard's End, 58
  The Longest Journey, 58
  A Passage to India, 58
  A Room with a View, 58
  Where Angels Fear to Tread, 58
Foulis, Andrew, 12, 15
Foulis, Robert, 5, 6, 12; *see also* Foulis Press
  bookshop, 12, 13
  Memorial of the Printers and Booksellers of Glasgow, Most Humbly Addressed to the Honourable House of Commons, 5
  printer to the University of Glasgow, 5

Foulis, Robert (*cont.*)
   student at Glasgow University, 12
Foulis Press, 12–15
   "Elzevirs of Britain," 13
   publishers of classic literature, 13–15
Franklin, Benjamin, 11, 29, 87
Fraser, James Baillie, 60
Frazer, Sir James George
   Golden Bough, 7
   Totemism, 101
free trade, 4, 51
Freeland, William
   A Birth Song and Other Poems, 104

Galsworthy, John
   Forsyte novels, 73
Galt, John, 57, 59, 76, 85
   The Spaewife, 102
   The Stolen Child, 60
Gaskell, Mrs. Elizabeth, 61, 62, 64, 65
   Cousin Phillis, 62, 65
   A Dark Night's Work, 62
   Life of Charlotte Brontë, 61
   Mary Barton, 61, 62
   North and South, 62
   Round the Sofa, 62
   Sylvia's Lovers, 62
   Wives and Daughters, 62
Gay, John
   The Beggar's Opera, 14
Genlis, Madame de, 9, 48
   The Knights of the Swan, or The Court of Charlemagne, 25
"Geoffrey Crayon, Gentleman," 18, *see* Irving, Washington
Gibbon, Edward, 11, 94
   Decline and Fall of the Roman Empire, 9, 11

Gissing, George, 78
   Introduction to the *Works of Charles Dickens*, 78; *see also* Blackie & Son
   The Private Papers of Henry Ryecroft, 38
"Glasgow style," 105, 107, 111; *see also* Gowans and Gray
King, Jessie M., 107
Godwin, Catherine Grace, 31
   Reine Canziani: A Tale of Modern Greece, 31
Godwin, William
   Caleb Wiliams, 24
   Mandeville. A Tale of the Seventeenth Century in England, 31
Goethe, Johann Wolfgang von, 57, 95
   Faust, 18, 57
   Poems and Ballads, 57
   Theory of Colours, 21
Goldsmith, Oliver, 72, 77, 78, 87, 94, 102, 109
   History of the Earth and Animated Nature, 39, 102
   History of Rome, 103
   The Vicar of Wakefield, 49
Gowans, Adam, 104
   printer and bookbinder, 104
Gowans, Adam Luke, 104, 105, 110
   art book publisher, 104–09
   editor, 110, 111
   head librarian of Glasgow School of Art, 105
   Lyric Masterpieces by Living Authors, 110
   A Treasury of English Verse, 110
Gowans, Charles, 104
Gowans and Gray, 20, 104–12
   emphasis on visual arts, 105–07

Gowans and Gray (*cont.*)
  and Glasgow style, 105, 107
  Gowans's Art Books, 105–06
  Gowans's International Library, 108
  The Hundred Best series, 108-1
    Chinese Fairy Tales told in English by Herbert A. Giles, 108–09
  international influence of, 111–12
  and Jessie M. King, 107–08
Graffigny, Françoise de, Madame, 9
Graham, Archibald Hamilton
  Poems, 104
Grove's *Dictionary of Music*, 2, 66
Gray, David
  The Luggie and other Poems, 104
Gray, Thomas, 14

Hall, Basil
  Account of a Voyage of Discovery to the West Coast of Corea and the Great Loo-Choo Island in the Japan Sea, 36
  Extracts from a Journal Written on the Coasts of Chile, Peru, and Mexico in the Years 1820, 1821, 1822, 36
Hall, David, 11
Hamilton, Janet
  Poems and Ballads, 104
  Poems, Sketches and Essays, 104
Hardy, Thomas, 58, 73, 92, 96; *see also* Macmillan
  Complete Works in Prose and Verse, 96
  The Dynasts, 96
  Far from the Madding Crowd, 65
  A Laodicean, 96
  The Mayor of Casterbridge, 96
  Tess of the D'Urbervilles, 96
  Wessex Tales, 96
  The Woodlanders, 96

Haweis, Thomas
  The Evangelical Expositor, or A Commentary on the Holy Bible, 75
Hawthorne, Nathaniel, 41, 77, 78, 79, 94
Hazlitt, William, 28, 50, 51, 76, 77
  Table-Talk, 50
Hedderwick, James
  The Villa by the Sea and other Poems, 104
Heine, Heinrich, 95
  Harzreise, 79
  Poems and Ballads of Heinrich Heine, 57
Hemans, Felicia, 72
Herrick, Robert, 71, 76, 77, 109
Heywood, Thomas, 76
Hogg, James, 57, 59
  "The Ettrick Shepherd," 60
  "Prayer of a Dying Soldier on the Field of Waterloo," 33
  Winter Evening Tales collected among the Cottagers of the South of Scotland, 102
Holloway, Thomas, 16
Homer, 13, 14
  The Iliad, 25, 80
  The Odyssey, 25
Hood, Thomas, 76, 85, 109
Howie, John
  Biographia Scoticana or Scots Worthies, 39
Howitt, Mary, 60
Hughes, Thomas, 92; *see also* Macmillan
  Tom Brown's School Days, 91
Hugo, Victor, 45, 77
  The Hunchback of Notre Dame, 25
  Les Misérables, 41

The Slave King/Bug Jargal, 60
Toilers of the Sea, 41
Humboldt, Alexander von, 29, 102;
    see also Oliver and Boyd
Ansichten der Natur, 102
Relation historique du Voyage aux régions équinoxiales du Nouveau Continent 1799–1804, 102
Vues des Cordillères et monuments des peuples indigènes de l'Amérique, 102
Hume, David, 76, 94
    co-founder of the Scottish Enlightenment, 12, 23
    Essays and Treatises, 8
    friend of Andrew Millar, 8
    friend of William Strahan, 11
    History of England, 8
    member of the Poker Club, 29
Hunt, Leigh, 51, 60, 76, 84
    Imagination and Fancy; or, Selections from the English Poets with an Essay in Answer to the Question What is Poetry, 61
Hunter, Henry
    translator of Lavater's *Essays in Physiognomy,* 15; *see also* John Murray
Hurst, Robinson & Co., 7, 31, 48, 49
Hutcheson, Francis, 12, 13

Irving, Washington, 19, 45, 76
    Bracebridge Hall, 18
    Geoffrey, Crayon, Gentleman, pseudonym of, 18
    Life and Voyages of Christopher Columbus, 20
    Tales of a Traveller, 18
    Tales of the Alhambra, 24

"Written in the Deepdene Album," 63

James, Henry, 92, 94, 95
    Daisy Miller, 66
    Washington Square, 66
James, William, 44
James Ballantyne & Co., 32, 46–49
    Novelist's Library, 48–49
        authors and titles reproduced, 48–49
John Ballantyne & Co., 32; *see also* Archibald Constable & Co.; Scott, Sir Walter
    collaborations, 49
    Edinburgh Annual Register, 33, 46–47
        Burke, Edmund, editor, 46
    financial troubles, 32, 48
    and Sir Walter Scott, 47
John Murray, 15–22; *see also* Murray, John; Murray, John II; Murray, John III; Murray, John IV
    Murray's Colonial and Home Library, 21
        George Borrow's *The Bible in Spain,* 21, 31
        Thomas Campbell's *British Poets,* 21
        Charles Darwin's *Beagle* travel journals, 21
        Herman Melville's *Omoo, Typee,* 21
    and Murray's Family Library series, 20, 21
    Murray's Magazine, 22
    publisher of the *Quarterly Review,* 19
    relationship with the D'Israeli family, 15, 18

INDEX

John Murray (*cont.*)
   and *The Representative*, 20
   sometime publisher of Jane Austen, 17, 19
Johnson, Samuel, 14, 94
   Dictionary, 8
   A Journey to the Western Islands of Scotland, 9
   Lives of the Most Eminent English Poets, 9
   Rasselas, 49
   The Works of English Poets, 16
Johnstone, Charles
   The Adventures of a Guinea, 49
Julius Caesar
   De Bello Gallico (*Commentaries on the Gallic War*), 54
   Opera Omnia, 24

Keats, John, 51, 76, 93, 109
   The Complete Works of Keats, 107
   Endymion, 52
Kempis, Thomas à
   The Imitation of Christ, 70
Kincaid, Alexander, 22
King, Jessie M., 107
Kingsley, Rev. Charles, 45, 73, 77, 90, 91, 92, 100; *see also* Macmillan
   "Cheap Clothes and Nasty," 90
   Glaucus, Or the Wonders of the Shore, 90
   Hereward the Wake, 91
   Hypatria, 91
   Phaeton, or Loose Thoughts for Loose Thinkers, 90
   The Water Babies, 73, 90
   Westward Ho!, 90
Kingston, W. H. G.
   On the Banks of the Amazon, or A Boy's Journal of his Adventures in the Tropical Wilds of South America, 42
   Twice Lost: A Story of Shipwreck and of Adventure in the Wilds of Australia, 42
   The Wanderers, or Adventures in the Wilds of Trinidad and up the Orinoco, 42
Kipling, Rudyard, 96; *see also* Macmillan
   Barrack-Room Ballads, 96
   Captains Courageous, 97
   His Private Honor, 96
   The Jungle Book, 96
   Just So Stories, 97
   Kim, 96
   The Kipling Reader, 97
   Life's Handicap, 96
   The Light that Failed, 96
   Puck of Pooks Hill, 97
   Second Jungle Book, 96
   Soldiers Three, 96
   Stalky & Co., 97
   Wee Willie Winkie, 96

Lamb, Charles, 72, 76, 77, 109
Lander, John
   Adventures in the Niger, 20
Lander, Richard
   Adventures in the Niger, 20
Lavater, Johann Kasper, 15
   Essays in Physiognomy, 15
   success of, 16
Law, William,
   Remarks, 89
Le Sage, Alain-René, 14
   The Devil upon Two Sticks, 25, 49
   Gil Blas, 49

Lewes, George Henry, 63, 65
   and *The Cornhill*, 63
   and George Eliot, 53, 63
Leyden, John, 27; *see also* Archibald Constable
   editor of *The Scots Magazine and Edinburgh Literary Miscellany*, 27
Licensing of the Press Act of 1662, 3
Livingstone, David
   Missionary Travels, 21
Locke, John, 10, 14, 87
Lockhart, John Gibson, 2, 17, 20; *see also* John Murray
   editor of Murray's Family Library, 20
   editor of *Quarterly Review*, 17
   Life of Napolean Buonaparte, 20
Longfellow, Henry Wadsworth, 45, 72, 77, 80, 92, 93, 95
Lord Byron, *see* Byron, George Gordon
Lyttelton, George
   Dialogues of the Dead, 16

Macfarquhar, Colin, 1, 101
   and *Encyclopaedia Britannica*, 1
Mackenzie, Henry, 11
   Julia de Roubigné, 49
   The Man of Feeling, 19, 49
   The Man of the World, 49
Mackintosh, Charles Rennie, 79
   Hill House, 79
Mackintosh, Sir James, 28
   Vindiciae Gallicae, 28
MacLehose, James, 89, 103–04
   bookseller to Glasgow University, 103
   friend of Alexander Macmillan, 93
   friend of Daniel Macmillan, 88, 103
   Glasgow University printer and publisher, 103
   publisher of Margaret Oliphant, 103
   titles of note, 103–04
Macmillan, 88–100
   bookshop, 90
   Coventry Patmore's *Children's Garland*, 93
   English Classics, 94
   English Men of Letters, 94, 95
      authors presented, 94
   Globe Library, 93, 94
   Golden Treasury Series, 93
      famous contributors, 93
   London branch, 91
      Tobacco Parliaments, 92
      participants, 91
   H. G. Wells and, 97
   Macmillan's Magazine, 92, 96
      famous contributors, 92
   as publisher of English literature, 95
   publisher of Rev. Charles Kingsley, 90–91, 100
   publisher of Rudyard Kipling, 96
   publisher of Thomas Hardy, 96
Macmillan, Alexander, 88, 97
   bookseller, 89
   friendship with Alfred Tennyson, 95
   friendship with James MacLehose, 89
   friendship with Matthew Arnold, 92, 96, 99
   and Globe Editions, 93
   publisher of Palgrave's *Golden Treasury of the Best Songs and*

Macmillan, Alexander (*cont.*)
    Lyrical Poems in the English Language, 92
Macmillan, Daniel, 88
    bookseller, 88, 89   illness of, 88
Macpherson, James
    Fingal, 10
Mandeville, Bernard
    Fable of the Bees, 89
Mansfield, Katherine
    The Garden Party and other stories, 38
Manzoni, Alessandro
    The Betrothed, 25
Marmontel, Jean-François
    Contes moraux, 16
Marvell, Andrew, 76
Maturin, Charles Robert, 31, 76
    The Albigenses: A Romance, 31
    Melmoth The Wanderer, 31
    Woman, or Pour et Contre, 31
Maurice, F. D., 89
    friend to Rev. Charles Kingsley, 90
    The Kingdom of Christ, 89
    "Prophet" to the Macmillans, 90
McEuen, James, 8
McMurray, John, *see* Murray, John
McQueen, James
    Narrative of the Political and Military Events of 1815, 74
Meldrum, David Storrar, 55
Melville, Herman, 73
    Omoo, 21; *see also* Murray's Colonial and Home Library
    Typee, 21; *see also* Murray's Colonial and Home Library
Meredith, George, 95
    The Adventures of Harry Richmond, 65
    The Amazing Marriage, 37
    "Chillianwallah," 85
Meynell, Alice, 78

London Impressions, 38
Millar, Andrew, 1, 7, 8–9, 10, 22
    bookseller, 8
    fight against pirated material, 4, 9
    partner, Thomas Cadell, 4
    publisher and friend of David Hume, 8
    publisher of Henry Fielding, 8, 10
    publisher of Tobias Smollett, 8
Millar, John, 13, 29
    Observations on the Distinction of Ranks in Society, 16
Millar, William, 22
Millar v. Kincaid, 9
Millar v. Taylor, 9
Milman, Henry Hart
    History of the Jews, 20
Milton, John, 8, 14, 71, 72, 76, 77, 93, 94, 109
Mitford, Mary Russell, 60
Montgomery, James, 71
    editor of *The Christian Poet,* 71; *see also* William Collins
Moore, Thomas, 17, 18, 28, 72
    Letters & Journals of Lord Byron, with Notices of his Life, 17
More, Sir Thomas, 14, 71
Morley, John, 94, 95
    editor of *The Cornhill,* 94
    English Men of Letter Series, 94; *see also* Macmillan
    reader for Macmillan, 97
Morris, Talwin, 78–79; *see also* Blackie & Son
    art director/book designer for Blackie & Sons, 78
    award-winning designs, 79
    examples, 79
Mühlbach, Luise, popular German writer of historical fiction, 41

INDEX

Murray, John, 15, 50
   bookseller, 15, 58
   founder of publishing house, 15
   friend of Isaac D'Israeli, 15
   and prejudice against Scottish booksellers, 15
   publisher of Johann Kaspar Lavater, 15, 16
   as publisher of literature, 16
   scientific and medical publisher, 16
Murray, John II, 7, 16–17
   friend of Lord Byron, 17
   friend of Isaac D'Israeli, 18
   friend of Washington Irving, 18
   friend of Sir Walter Scott, 17
   publisher of Jane Austen, 17, 19
   and the *Quarterly Review*, 19
   and *The Representative* (newspaper), 20
   success of, 16
Murray, John III, 19
Murray, John IV, 22
   acquisition of Smith Elder & Co., 22
   publisher to Queen Victoria, 22

Nature, 2
Nelson, Thomas, Jr., 39, 40, 41; *see also* Thomas Nelson
Nelson, Thomas, Sr., 38, 40; *see also* Thomas Nelson
Nelson, William, 40, 42; *see also* Thomas Nelson
Nichol, John
   The Death of Themistocles, a Dramatic Fragment, and other Poems, 104
   Hannibal: A Historical Drama, 104

O'Casey, Sean, 100
Oliver and Boyd, 70, 101–03
   Albyn's Anthology or A Select Collection of the Melodies and Local Poetry Peculiar to Scotland and the Isles, hitherto unpublished, 102
   Edinburgh Cabinet Library, 102
   "favourite song" collections, 102
   history books published, 102–03
   reprints, 103
Oliphant, Margaret, 84, 85
   Effie Ogilvie, The Story of a Young Life, 103
   A House Divided Against Itself, 85
Oliver, Thomas, 101
Otway, Thomas, 14

Pater, Walter
   Marius the Epicurean, 96
Patmore, Coventry, 77, 92; *see also* Macmillan
   editor, *The Children's Garland from the Best Poets*, 93
Payn, James, 85; *see also* W. & R. Chambers
   editor of *Chambers's Journal*, 84
   editor of *The Cornhill*, 85
   The Family Scapegrace, 85
pirated editions, 3, 4, 9, 21, 22, 23
Pope, Alexander, 14, 71, 72, 77
Pringle, John, 11
printers, 2, 3, 7, 15
Prior, Matthew, 14
proofreader, 14
protectionism, 4

Quarterly Review, 7, 17, 19, 51, 59
Queen Victoria, 22
   Leaves from the Journal of our Life in the Highlands, 65
   The Letters of Queen Victoria, 22

Queen Victoria (*cont.*)
   More Leaves from the Journal of our Life in the Highlands from 1862 to 1882, 65
   publishers to, 22, 37, 65

Radcliffe, Ann
   Castles of Athlin and Dunbayne, 49
   The Italian, 49
   The Mysteries of Udolpho, 49
   The Romance of the Forest, 49
   The Sicilian Romance, 49
Reade, Charles
   Put Yourself in His Place, 65
reading public, 6, 35, 76, 80
Reeve, Clara
   The Old English Baron, 49
Reid, Thomas, 23
   Inquiry into the Human Mind: on the Philosophy of Common Sense, 26
Richardson, Samuel, 49
   Clarissa, 49
   Pamela, or Virtue Rewarded, 49, 75
   Sir Charles Grandison, 49
Richmond, George, 61; see also Brontë, Charlotte
Rivington, John, 4, 58
Robertson, William, 26
   History of Scotland during the Reigns of Queen Mary and King James VI, 8, 39
Robinson, George, 23
Rollin, Charles
   Histoire ancienne, 74
Rossetti, Christina, 80, 92, 95, 107
Rousseau, Jean-Jacques, 46
   La Nouvelle Héloïse (Julia, or The New Eloisa), 25
   price of, 25
Rowe, Nicholas, 14
Ruskin, John, 60, 64, 65, 77, 107; see also Smith, George Murray
   Fors Clavigera, 60
   Modern Painters, 60
   The Seven Lamps of Architecture, 60
   The Stones of Venice, 60
   Unto this Last, 60

Sallust
   Bellum Catalinae, 24
   Bellum Jugurthinum, 24
Sand, George, 46, 95
Schiller, Friedrich
   Der Geisterseher (The Ghost-Seer), 25
   History of the Thirty Years' War, 36
   The Robbers, 25
Schlegel, Friedrich
   Lectures on the History of Literature, 57
Scott, Sir Walter, 7, 17, 18, 19, 20, 26, 28, 30, 44, 46, 93, 94
   The Abbot, 33
   The Antiquary, 33
   The Black Dwarf, 50
   The Fortunes of Nigel, 33
   Guy Mannering, 33
   Ivanhoe, 33
   Kenilworth, 33
   The Lady of the Lake, 32, 81
   The Lay of the Last Minstrel, 31
   Marmion, 32
   Minstrelsy of the Scottish Border, 31
   The Monastery, 33
   and a *Novelist's Library*, 48, 49
   Peveril of the Peak, 33
   The Pirate, 33
   Quenhoo Hall: A Legendary Romance, being a History of Times Past, 32

Quentin Durward, 33
Redgauntlet, 33
Rob Roy, 33
Sir Tristrem, 31
St. Ronan's Well, 33
Tales of the Crusaders, 33
Tales of My Landlord (Old Mortality), 50
Waverley, 32
Woodstock, or The Cavalier. A tale of the Year Sixteen Hundred and Fifty-One, 33
and Arnold Constable, 30–33
critical review in *The Edinburgh Review*, 32, 46, 47
and the Friday Club, 29
and John Ballantyne & Co., 32, 34, 46–48
Scottish Court of Session, 9
Scottish Enlightenment, 12, 14, 23
Shaftesbury, Third Earl of, 14
Shakespeare, William, 3, 14, 71, 72, 93, 109
Shaw, George Bernard
Ann Veronica, 99
Cashel Byron's Profession, 97
The Doctor's Dilemma, 38
The History of Mr. Polly, 99
Immaturity, 58, 97
In the Days of the Comet, 99
The Irrational Knot, 97
Man and Superman, 38
The New Macchiavelli, 99
The Passionate Friends, 99
Tungo-Bungay, 99
An Unsocial Socialist, 97
"Wagner in Bayreuth," 98
The Wife of Sir Isaac Harman, 99
The World Set Free: A Story of Mankind, 99
and Macmillan, 97, 98
Shelley, Mary Wollstonecraft
Frankenstein or the Modern Prometheus, 24
Shelley, Percy Bysshe, 28, 48, 50, 51, 52, 72, 80, 89, 94, 109
Prometheus Unbound, 50
Smellie, William, 1, 23, 101; see also A. & C. Black
co-founder of the Royal Society of Edinburgh, 2
co-founder of the Society of Antiquaries of Scotland, 2
Smith, Adam
Theory of Moral Sentiments, 10
The Wealth of Nations with a Life of the Author; also a View of the Doctrine of Smith, 9, 10
Smith, Charlotte, 9
Smith, George, 58
apprenticeship, 58
early employment, 58
Smith, George Murray, 58
and Charlotte Brontë, 60, 61
and *Dictionary of National Biography*, 66
early employment, 60
friendship with John Ruskin, 60
Smith & Elder, 58–59
booksellers and stationers, 58
and East India Company, 58, 59
and English literature, 58–59
publishers, 59
Smith, Elder, & Co., 59–66
The Cornhill, 62–65
De Luxe series, 65
giftbooks, 59
Chronicles of London Bridge, 59
Views of Calcutta, engraved by Robert Havell, 59

Smith, Elder, & Co. (*cont.*)
  Illustrated Library, 65
  Library of Romance, 59–60; *see also* Hugo, Victor; Galt, John
  Pocket series, 65
  Popular series, 65
Smollett, Tobias, 8, 9, 14, 16, 87
  Count Fathom, 49
  Humphrey Clinker, 49
  Peregrine Pickle, 24, 49
  Roderick Random, 49
  Sir Launcelot Greaves, 49
  translator of Cervantes's *Don Quixote*, 8, 49
  translator of Le Sage's *Gil Blas*, 8, 49
Somerville, Dr. Thomas, 11
  History of Great Britain during the Reign of Queen Anne, 11
Southey, Robert, 59
  Life of Nelson, 20
  "Peter of Barnet," 33
Spencer, Edmund, 71, 77, 94
Spottiswoode, Andrew, 11; *see also* William Strahan
Staël, Germaine, Madame de
  Corinne, or Italy, 25, 30
  De l'Allemagne, 18
  Delphine, 30
Stationers' Company, 3, 9, 22
Statute of Anne of 1710, 3
Steele, Richard, 14
Stephen, Leslie, 65
  editor of *The Cornhill*, 65–66
  editor of *Dictionary of National Biography*, 66
Sterne, Laurence, 77, 80
  A Sentimental Journey, 49
  Complete Works, 16
  Sermons of Mr. Yorick, 10
  Tristram Shandy, 49

Stevenson, Robert Louis, 57
Stewart, Dugald, 22
  Collected Works, 37
Stewart, Patrick, 59
Stoker, Bram
  Dracula, 38
Strachan, William, *see* Strahan, William
Strahan, Andrew, 11
  successor to William Strahan, 11
Strahan, William, 10–12
  apprentice of Andrew Millar, 9
  and Benjamin Franklin, 11
  collaboration with Thomas Caddell, 10
  famous titles produced, 10–11, 12
  as compositor, 10
  friendships with authors, 11
  printer, 10
    for Andrew Millar, 10
    for Thomas Becket, 10
  portrait by Joshua Reynolds, 11
  posthumous publisher of Andrew Millar's titles, 10–11
Strutt, Joseph, 32
Swift, Jonathan, 72, 77, 78, 79
  Gulliver's Travels, 49
Symonds, John Addington, 64, 94
Symons, Arthur, 110
  William Blake, 38

T. & A. Constable, 37
Tacitus, 14, 25
Tagore, Rabindranath, 100
  Gitanjali, 100
Tasso, Torquato, 14
Tennyson, Alfred, Lord, 45, 51, 72, 77, 80
  "Tithonus," 63
Thackeray, William Makepeace, 45, 52, 62, 63, 64, 65, 66

The Adventures of Philip, 63
Denis Duval, 65
English Humourists of the Eighteenth Century, 62
Henry Esmond, 62
The Kickleburys on the Rhine, 62
Lovel the Widower, 62
The Roundabout Papers, 62
The Rose and the Ring, 62
and *The Cornhill*, 62, 63
and George Murray Smith, 61
Thomas Nelson, 38–46
   books for children, 41–43
   commercial considerations, 38, 41
   first New York branch office, 6, 40
   focus on English-language classics, 38, 41, 46
   French branch, 45–46
   Hope Park factory, 40
   New Century Library, 44, 45
     book prices, 45
   number-publications, 38
   onetime publisher of Jane Austen, 45
   production and distribution techniques, 39
   renamed "Thomas Nelson and Sons," 40
   schoolbooks, 44–45
     Royal Readers series, 44–45
   Sixpenny Classics/Nelson Classics, 45
Thomson, James, 6, 8, 72
   The Seasons, 8
Thomson, John, 38
   Through China with a Camera, with over 100 illustrations, 38
Thomson, Richard
   Chronicles of London Bridge, 59
Timperley, C. H., 1
   Dictionary of Printers and Printing, 37
Tolstoy, Leo, 45, 73

Treaty of Union, 3, 7, 112
Trollope, Anthony, 45, 53, 54
   The Fixed Period, 54
   Framley Parsonage, 63
   Linda Tressel, 54
   Nina Balatka, 53, 54
   The Small House at Allington, 65
   and *The Cornhill*, 62, 63
   and George Murray Smith, 62, 64
Trotter, A. M.
   A Manual of English Grammar, 72
Tucker, Charlotte Maria, 43
   The Silver Casket, or The World and its Wiles, 43
   Stories Illustrating the Proverbs, 43
   Stories from Jewish History, 43
   The Thorn in the Conscience and Other Stories, 43
   The Young Pilgrims: A Tale Illustrative of 'The Pilgrim's Progress,' 43

Vanbrugh, John, 14
Views of Calcutta, engraved by Robert Havell, 60
   aquatints, 60; *see also* Fraser, James Baillie
Voltaire, 14, 16

W. & R. Chambers, 80–88: *see also* Chambers, Robert; Chambers, William
   Chambers' Edinburgh Journal, 82–83
     editor, James Payn, 85
     famous contributors, 84, 85, 86
     opening address, 83
     readership of, 83, 84
     renaming of, 84
   Chambers's Educational Course, 86
   Chambers's Encyclopaedia: A Dictionary of Useful Knowledge, 87

W. & R. Chambers (*cont.*)
- *Cyclopaedia of English Literature: A History, Critical and Biographical, of British Authors, in All Departments of Literature, Illustrated by Specimens of Their Writings*, 87
- *Gazeteer of Scotland*, 82
- *Information for the People*, 86
- People's Editions, 86, 87
  - famous contributors, 87

Walpole, Horace
- *Castle of Otranto*, 49

Walpole, Hugh, 100

Wells, H. G., 44, 58, 73, 97, 99; *see also* Macmillan
- *Food of the Gods*, 99
- *The Island of Dr. Moreau*, 99
- *Kipps*, 99
- *Love and Mr. Lewisham*, 98
- *The Sea Lady: A Tissue of Moonshine*, 99
- *Tales of Space and Time*, 99
- *The Time Machine*, 99
- *Twelve Stories and a Dream*, 99
- *The War of the Worlds*, 99
- *The World Set Free: A Story of Mankind*, 99
- *When the Sleeper Awakes*, 99

Wilberforce, William,
- Abolition of Slavery Act of 1833, 69
- *A Practical Review of the Prevailing System of Professed Christians in the Higher and Middle Classes in This Country Contrasted with Real Christianity*, 69
- Slave Trade Act of 1807, 69

William Blackwood and Sons, 49–58; *see also* John Blackwood, William Blackwood
- Ancient Classics for English Readers, 53
- co-publishing, 50
- *Edinburgh Monthly Magazine*, later *Blackwood's Edinburgh Magazine*, 50–52
- historical and religious works, 50
- as publisher of fine literature, 52
- travel and exploration texts, 50

William Collins, 66–7
- *The Christian Poet*, 71
  - major English poets included in series, 71
- Novel Library, 73
- Penny Library series, 73
- publisher of schoolbooks, 70–71, 73
- Select Christian Biography, Intended for Youth, 70
  - *Pious Grandson, The History of James Anderson*, 70
  - *The Widow of Rosenheath, a Lesson of Piety*, 70
- Select Library of Christian Authors, 69
- *Select Practical Writings of John Knox*, 71
- and Thomas Chalmers, 68–70

Wilson, Alexander, 13
- *American Ornithology*, 37

Winckelmann, Johann Joachim, 13

Witherspoon, John
- *Treatises on Justification and Regeneration*, 70

Wordsworth, William, 18, 48, 51, 72, 93, 96, 109
- "The Stranger," 33

Yeats, W. B., 100, 110
Young, Edward
  Night Thoughts, 14

Zola, Emile
  Une Page d'amour, 46

www.ingramcontent.com/pod-product-compliance
Lightning Source LLC
Chambersburg PA
CBHW080926100426
42812CB00007B/2379